Study Guide to

Cat's Cradle

by Kurt Vonnegut

by Ray Moore

U.S. Army portrait of Pvt. Kurt Vonnegut, Jr. early 1940s.

This image is a work of a U.S. Army soldier taken as part of that person's official duties. As a work of the U.S. federal government the image is in the public domain.

Preface:

A Study Guide is an *aid* to the close reading of a text; it is *never* a substitute for reading the text. This novel deserves to be read *reflectively*, and the aim of this guide is to facilitate such a reading. The study guide questions have *no* answers provided. This is a deliberate choice. I am writing for readers who want to come to *their own conclusions* about the text and not simply to be told what to think about it by someone else. Even 'suggested' answers would limit the *exploration of the text* by readers themselves which is my primary aim.

In the classroom, I found that students frequently came up with answers that I had not even considered, and, not infrequently, that they expressed their ideas better than I could have done. The point of this Guide is to *open up* the text, not to close it down by providing 'ready-made answers.' Teachers do not need their own set of predetermined answers in order effectively to evaluate the responses of their students.

Acknowledgements

As always, I am indebted to the work of many critics. Where I am conscious of having taken an idea or a phrase from a particular author, I cite the source in the text: failure to do so is an omission which I will immediately correct if it is drawn to my attention. I believe that all quotations used in the book and other sources fall under the definition of 'fair use'. Once again, if I am in error on any quotation, I will immediately remove it if it is drawn to my attention. The image of a cat's cradle is in the public domain (source Wikimedia Commons),

Spoiler alert!

If you are reading the novel for the first time, you may wish to go straight to the Study Guide and Questions section and come back to the introductory sections later since they do explain everything that happens in the novel, including the ending!

Contents

Introduction

Plot Summary:

The narrator, John, begins by describing his intention, when he was "a much younger man," to write a book titled *The Day the World Ended*. The book was "to be an account of what important Americans had done on the day when the first atomic bomb was dropped on Hiroshima, Japan" (1). Research takes John to Ilium to interview people about the late Dr. Felix Hoenikker who worked on, and was crucial to, the development of the bomb. John discovers a great deal about Hoenikker and his three children (Newt, Angela and Franklin) and about the scientific research facility in which Hoenikker worked. He also learns that Hoenikker's final project was *ice-nine*, a substance that would freeze water at normal temperatures. He is assured, however, that this was a purely theoretical study and that no *ice-nine* was ever produced. John's plans for the book never came to fruition.

Then, one Sunday reading a supplement in the New York *Sunday Times*, John discovers that Frank (who had disappeared from Ilium on the day of his father's funeral and was thought to be dead) is actually Major General Franklin Hoenikker, *Minister of Science and Progress in the Republic of San Lorenzo*. Either by chance or as "it was supposed to happen" (84), John is assigned to write a magazine story in San Lorenzo, a small island state in the Caribbean.

In the course of his research, John meets Newt, Angela and Franklin and learns that, on the day of their father's death, each of them took a portion of *ice-nine*. Angela's portion eventually found its way to the US government, Newt's to the government of the USSR, and Frank's to "Papa" Monzano, the dictator who rules San Lorenzo.

During a disastrous military display on the island, "Papa" Monzano's sample of *ice-nine* is released and very quickly every molecule of water on earth freezes. John and a few others on San Lorenzo manage to survive, but most of the islanders either die as a direct result of frozen water or commit mass suicide. The assumption is that much the same sequence of events has happened around the world.

Why Read this Book?

Up until the publication of his novel *Slaughterhouse Five* (1969), very few of Vonnegut's novels had been reviewed and most of them were out of print. Following the phenomenal popularity of *Slaughterhouse Five*, Vonnegut's subsequent books (novels, short stories and non-fiction) have always been reviewed, and (the last time I checked) all of them are still in print. For a writer of his post- World War II generation, particularly one as prolific as Vonnegut, this is a remarkable achievement.

That said, Vonnegut is not for everyone. His fiction is odd and quirky, and it takes some getting used to. I think it would be accurate to say that (with the obvious exception of *Slaughterhouse Five*), Vonnegut has something akin to cult status with readers. I do not recall his name ever having been linked with the Nobel Prize in Literature, but it really should have been.

Issues with this Book

There is sex in the novel, but no graphic descriptions of sex. There is violence in the novel (as you would expect from a book which includes the destruction of human life on the entire planet) but no graphic descriptions of violence. I think I remember the f… word coming up once.

The controversial element of Vonnegut's work has always been his blistering critique of what he saw as the betrayal of American values in the America of his day. Right-wing critics condemn him for his left-wing, socialist views. (I remember the Fox News 'obituary' on the occasion of Vonnegut's death as being the most shameful job of attacking a person's achievement that I can ever remember.)

Dramatis Personæ – Selective List of Characters

John (aka Jonah) – John, the narrator and protagonist of the novel, tells the reader that he once planned to write a book about the day the atomic bomb was dropped which he intended to call *The Day the World Ended*. His intention was to give an account of what "important Americans had done on the day when the first atomic bomb was dropped on Hiroshima, Japan" (1). His research on the late Dr. Felix Hoenikker, the Nobel Prize winning physicist who was generally regarded as one of the 'fathers' of the atom bomb, leads him ultimately to come into contact with all three of Hoenikker's children, Angela, Frank, and Newt. This, in turn, causes John to become involved with their plans to exploit their father's final scientific creation, *ice-nine*, a substance which can turn water to ice at normal temperatures.

The Hoenikker Family and Associates:

Felix Hoenikker – The late Nobel Prize winning physicist was a key member of the Manhattan Project which developed the atomic bomb. Dr Hoenikker appears to John to have been entirely preoccupied with his research: he had neither time for, nor interest in, his family or any other social contacts since he was emotionally indifferent to other people. He is repeatedly referred to as behaving like a child, and he seemed to regard his research as an intellectual game: he sees no distinction between researching the atomic bomb and researching the behavior of turtles. Both are abstract puzzles which he studies for their inherent interest. Asked what games he played to relax, he replied, "'Why should I bother with made-up games when there are so many real ones going on?'" (11). Hoenikker failed to see that scientific research could have catastrophic as well as benevolent effects; in fact, he was indifferent to implications his research could have for mankind. His last research was prompted by a Marine general who wanted a solution to the problem of mud which made military operations difficult. Hoenikker created of an isotope of water that he called *ice-nine* which would freeze water at atmospheric temperature. Shortly afterwards, Hoenikker died suddenly leaving no records of his research. On the day of his death, his children, Angela, Frank, and Newt secretly divided the only sample of *ice-nine* among themselves.

[In *Palm Sunday* (1981), Vonnegut identified the model for Felix Hoenikker as Irving Langmuir (1881-1957) winner of The Nobel Prize in Chemistry in 1932 "for his discoveries and investigations in surface chemistry" (The Nobel Foundation). "Langmuir had worked [at General Electric] with Vonnegut's [older] brother, Bernard Vonnegut" (1914-1997) (Wikipedia article).]

Emily Hoenikker - Dr. Hoenikker's beautiful wife died while giving birth to Newt probably as a result of injuries sustained in a prior car accident. Her husband showed her scant affection or concern either while she was alive or after her death. A year after she died, he had still not bought a tombstone to mark her grave, so Angela and Frank (Newt still being a baby) used some of his Nobel Prize money to buy an impressive marker for her grave.

Angela Hoenikker - Angela, the oldest of the Hoenikker children is over six feet tall, and physically unattractive. When John first sees her he describes her as "a horse-faced woman" (101). After her mother died giving birth to Newt, her husband pulled Angela out of high school to take care of the family: she led an unhappy life with no outside friends or interests other than playing the clarinet alone in her room. Angela convinced herself that her father was an unappreciated saint. After her father's death, Harrison C. Conners, a scientist involved with top secret weapons research for the U.S. government, paid a visit to the family home. Despite the fact that he was very handsome and Angela was certainly not attractive, the two were married within two weeks. We later learn that Angela traded her share of *ice-nine* to Conners in exchange for marrying her.

Harrison C. Conners - This handsome scientist, involved in top-secret weapons research for the U.S. government, married Angela Hoenikker in return for her portion of *ice-nine,* which he gave to the United States' weapons arsenal. Angela's marriage is not happy since Harrison is routinely unfaithful to her. He is still alive, but does not appear in the novel.

Franklin (Frank) Hoenikker - The second Hoenikker child (presumably named for the great scientist and politician Benjamin Franklin) is temperamentally antisocial like his father, except that his passion in his youth was model making rather than science. While he was in high school, he joined no clubs, and played no sports; the other kids called him, Secret Agent X-9 [which is actually very close to *ice-nine*!] because he was always acting like he was heading to a secret place. Much later on, John will discover that Frank did have a secret life in Ilium that he had good reason to keep secret. After disappearing from town immediately following his father's funeral, he innocently got himself involved in smuggling in Miami and is wanted by the Florida police, the FBI, and the Treasury Department for running stolen cars to Cuba. Arriving on San Lorenzo, Frank bought himself the title and position of Major General and *Minister of Science and Progress in the Republic of San Lorenzo* in return for giving *ice-nine* to the island's dictator "Papa" Monzano. When the dictator falls ill at a public ceremony, he names Frank as the next President of San Lorenzo. However, Frank has no wish to accept the responsibility of ruling the island and convinces John to become President in his place.

Newt Hoenikker - The youngest Hoenikker child (presumably named for the great scientist Sir Isaac Newton) is a well-formed, four-foot midget. His mother died giving birth to him. Newt dropped out of pre-med at Cornell and briefly found happiness when he became engaged to Zinka, a midget ballet dancer. Newt's sole form of self-expression seems to be his painting.

Zinka – Newt fell in love with this Ukrainian ballet dancer to whom he was briefly engaged. She turned out to be a Soviet spy who stole from him his portion of *ice-nine* which she took back to the Soviet Union.

Cat's Cradle by Kurt Vonnegut

Characters Associated with the Research Laboratory at Ilium:

The Breed Family:

Dr. Asa Breed - Dr. Hoenikker's supervisor at the Research Laboratory is interviewed by John when he is researching his book *The Day the World Ended*. The night before, Sandra, a prostitute, has told John that "everyone in Ilium was sure that Dr. Breed had been in love with Felix Hoenikker's wife … that most people thought Breed was the father of all three Hoenikker children" (28). The interview does not go well, however, because Dr. Breed concludes from John's questions that he believes scientists to be heartlessly indifferent to the plight of humanity. Breed describes Dr. Hoenikker's ideas for *ice-nine* but presents them as only conceptual with no actual outcome. He firmly denies the existence of *ice-nine*.

Dr. Breed's son – This unnamed character resigned from the research institute that his father heads on the day the bomb was dropped on Hiroshima and went to work for his uncle Marvin cutting stone for monuments.

Marvin Breed – Dr. Breed's brother owns the tombstone shop in Ilium. He provided the monument for Emily Hoenikker's grave which was paid for by the three children. He was in love with Emily. He also provided the modest monument for Dr. Hoenikker' grave.

Others:

Francine Pefko – As secretary to Dr. Nilsak Horvath at the Research Laboratory, she takes dictation without understanding what she is writing about. She states, "'it's just like a foreign language'" (34).

Naomi Faust – Dr. Breed's secretary shows John around Dr. Hoenikker's lab which remains unchanged since his death. Her surname reminds us of Faust who sold his soul to the Devil for unlimited knowledge and earthly pleasures. In serving Dr. Breed and the research institute, she has done the same thing.

Jack – John interviews the owner of Jack's Hobby Shop where Frank worked while he was in high school. Jack shows a lot of pride in the models that Frank produced there and is outwardly emotional when John raises the subject of Frank's supposed death. John will later learn from Frank that he went so frequently to the model shop because he was "'screwing Jack's wife every day'" which is why he fell asleep in school and never achieved his full potential (201).

Sherman Krebbs - While John is in Ilium researching his book *The Day the World Ended,* he allows Krebbs, a homeless poet, to live in his apartment for a couple of weeks. When he comes back, John finds that Krebbs has incurred hundreds of dollars in long distance phone calls, wrecked his apartment, and

6

killed his cat. John credits Krebbs for turning him away from a philosophy of nihilism and making him a more receptive target for Bokononism.

Characters Associated with San Lorenzo:

Characters in the History of San Lorenzo:

Lionel Boyd Johnson (aka **Bokonon**) – When he and Edward McCabe landed on San Lorenzo, they found a people ravaged by poverty and disease. They thought that they could turn the island into a utopian paradise. Soon convinced of the futility of their efforts, Johnson created the religion of Bokononism which used lies to make the islanders feel better about their atrocious lives. To make the religion attractive to the people, Johnson suggested that McCabe become the island dictator and persecute followers of the new religion. Thus, Bokonon reinvented himself as a prophet to the people, but in doing so became a fugitive on the island because his teachings were against the law. John becomes a follower of Bokononism after he travels to San Lorenzo to interview Julian Castle for a magazine article. John finally meets Bokonon at the end of the novel. Readers may miss the important detail that Johnson/Bokonon is black.

Edward McCabe - This deserter from the Marines, offered Lionel Boyd Johnson $500 to sail him from Haiti to Miami, but they were shipwrecked on San Lorenzo, which lacked a government at the time. Seeing the horrendous poverty and disease among the island residents, which was partly the result of the Castle Sugar Corporation's abusive labor practices, Johnson and McCabe set out to make the island into a utopia. Because Castle Sugar had never turned a profit on San Lorenzo, the company retreated without protest when McCabe and Johnson declared themselves in charge of the island. However, the two soon realized that no amount of legal and economic reform could improve the standard of living of the people, so they sought to create a society based on the Dynamic Tension between Bokononism, a religion based on lies which sought to comfort the island's citizens, and the civil forces, which sought to repress Bokononism. At Johnson's request, McCabe, now a dictator, outlawed Bokononism so that it would be more exciting and meaningful to its followers. The strain of playing their roles in this charade drove both Bokonon and McCabe a little insane. McCabe began actually executing people who were found to be followers of Bokononism on the hook (a gruesome form of public execution), though he never killed Bokonon because, without him, his own role as tyrant would be meaningless. Finally, he committed suicide naming his major-domo "Papa" Monzano as his successor.

Nestor Aamons - This Finnish architect, designed Julian Castle's charity hospital, the House of Hope and Mercy, on San Lorenzo. He was Mona's biological father.

The Hundred Martyrs to Democracy - After the bombing of Pearl Harbor, San Lorenzo declared war on Japan and Germany. The island conscripted one hundred soldiers who were put onto a ship bound for the United States, but a German submarine sank the ship just as it left the harbor of the capital Bolivar, killing all of the soldiers. They became known as the Hundred Martyrs to Democracy, and San Lorenzo created a national holiday in their memory.

Characters that John Encounters on San Lorenzo:

Julian Castle - John travels to San Lorenzo to interview Julian for a magazine article. The multi-millionaire was the owner of the unprofitable Castle Sugar Corporation. Having spent the first forty years of his life as an immoral playboy, he turned his attention to charity, building and running the House of Hope and Mercy a hospital in the Jungle for the next twenty years. A devout Bokononist, he administers the last rites to patients after they died and teaches Jonah a great deal about the practice of Bokononism on the island.

Philip Castle - Julian Castle's only child is the author of the book *San Lorenzo: The Land, the History, the People* which John reads on the flight to San Lorenzo. He is also the owner of a hotel in which John first stays on San Lorenzo, the Casa Mona. Philip and Mona grew up together and were briefly engaged.

Horlick and Claire Minton - John meets the newly appointed American ambassador to San Lorenzo and his wife on the flight to the island. They introduced him to Philip Castle's book about the island, which gave John his first information about Bokononism. At the official commemoration of the Hundred Martyrs to Democracy, Horlick delivers a spontaneous speech against the murderous consequences of patriotism and nationalism. He declares that all soldiers who die in war are "murdered children." Shortly after that he dies (along with just about everyone else) in the accidental explosion that devastates the castle and releases *ice-nine* which destroys life on earth.

H. Lowe and Hazel Crosby - John meets these husband and wife Hoosiers (natives of Indiana) on the plane to San Lorenzo. They are traveling to San Lorenzo to investigate the possibility of moving their bicycle manufacturing business to the island because H. Lowe finds U.S. labor regulations too restrictive. They fully approve of the harshness of the island's dictator and tell John about the hook, the only form of punishment used on the island, which they credit for the fact that crime is almost non-existent.

Miguel "Papa" Monzano – The dictator of the small island republic of San Lorenzo is old and sick by the time John first meets him. He employed Frank as a Major General in exchange for *ice-nine* and intended that Frank should succeed him after his death. Finally, near death from cancer, Monzano committed suicide by swallowing ice-nine.

Mona Aamons Monzano - The stunningly beautiful adopted daughter of "Papa" Monzano was actually the child of Nestor Aamons, a Finnish architect who died prior to her birth, and a woman native to San Lorenzo. Monzano adopted her to raise his popularity, and he turned her into an erotic national symbol. Mona is a devout Bokononist and *The Books of Bokonon* predict that she will marry the next President. When John sees her for the first time she is eighteen and he falls hopelessly in love with her. Mona, however, is about to marry Frank who convinces John to become the successor to "Papa" Monzano as President of San Lorenzo by telling him that, if he agrees, Mona will marry him. Finally, Mona commits suicide by swallowing *ice-nine* after it kills almost all life on earth.

Dr. Vox Humana – This self-styled Christian minister appears to have got his qualifications from the Western Hemisphere University of the Bible in Little Rock, Arkansas, having seen their advertisement in *Popular Mechanics* magazine. A talented caricaturist, he is responsible for the representation of tyrants which are the targets for the San Lorenzo Air Force on the Day of the Hundred Martyrs of Democracy. He comes "to administer Christian rites as he understood them" to the dying "Papa" Monzano but is turned away when "Papa" reveals that he is a Bokononist.

Dr. Schlichter von Koenigswald - This former S.S. officer served at Auschwitz for six years and was responsible for thousands of deaths. As penance for his war crimes, he became a member of Julian's staff at the House of Hope and Mercy. He is "Papa" Monzano's personal doctor. After Monzano commits suicide by swallowing ice-nine, Dr. von Koenigswald gets some of the substance on his hands and when he tries to wash them, he dies instantly because the *ice-nine* freezes the water in his body.

Genre

Morse states that "Vonnegut's work escapes easy classification." He lists the following genres that might apply to Vonnegut's early novels (of which *Cat's Cradle* is one): "science fiction, black comedy, satire, schizophrenic fiction, fabulation, fantasy, and so forth" (24).

Satire

The most obvious genre to describe *Cat's Cradle* is satire which may be defined as, "a literary work that uses biting wit, irony, and/or sarcasm to expose, discredit and hold up to scorn and ridicule human vices and follies" (adapted from Merriam-Webster). In 1729, a work by satirist Jonathan Swift (most famous as the author of *Gulliver's Travels*, 1726) was published anonymously. Its full title was *A Modest Proposal For preventing the Children of Poor People From being a Burthen to Their Parents or Country, and For making them Beneficial to the Publick*. In it Swift ironically suggests that impoverished Irish peasants might sell their young children as food for rich gentlemen and ladies, thus solving at a stroke the related problems of overly-large families and poverty. The target of Swift's satire was the social engineering approach to 'improving' society so popular in his day, and the inhumane attitudes of the British government towards the poor (and particularly the Irish poor). Vonnegut is writing, then, in the tradition of Jonathan Swift.

Morse singles out *Cat's Cradle* as the early novel in which "the bitterest satire occurs" (21). This being so, it is very easy to see what aspects of life in the mid-twentieth century (and more particularly of American life in this period) are being satirized than it is to see what is *not* being satirized. In this novel, the positive values evident in other Vonnegut novels and (particularly) in his non-fiction and his speeches, are hard to identify. Again, Morse writes:

> Vonnegut from his vantage point of the second half of the twentieth century focuses on the failure of America to keep its promises, especially those relating to social justice, while achieving far too many trivial objectives … Vonnegut used his fame to further the public good in becoming a spokesman of conscience against "show-biz wars," racism, amoral profiteering, drug abuse, meaningless work, and public, corporate, and private abuses of power. (Morse xiv-xv)

In *Cat's Cradle*, the reader feels secure in knowing what Vonnegut is against, but much less clear about what he is offering as counter or normative values.

If we ask what aspects of his time are the targets of Vonnegut's satire, we might be tempted to reply, "Everything!" Since that is not particularly helpful, we may list (in a rough order of importance): man's developing technological capacity for mass destruction (including the Cold War, and the role of scientists, politicians and the military industrial complex); religion (specifically, but not exclusively, Christianity); capitalist neo-colonialism (including the outsourcing of production and American exceptionalism); parenting (specifically the failure of parents to love and nurture their children); racism; and the economic disparity between rich and poor (including trickle-down economics). If we ask what positive values Vonnegut offers in this novel, Morse suggests (21) that they are encapsulated in this dialogue from the Bokononist creation myth:

> Man blinked [when he saw the earth God had
> created]. "What is the purpose of all this? He
> asked politely.
> "Everything must have a purpose?" asked God.
> "Certainly," said man.
> "Then I leave you to think of one for all this,"
> said God.
> And He went away. (265)

It is a pity that Bokononism does not show people that there is no 'secret' to life, because the novel makes it clear that there is not – no divine will, no scientific breakthrough, no single political ideology. Stop looking for simplistic formulas that promise to save your existence from meaninglessness, the novel says: you give life meaning by acting meaningfully – by loving and caring and helping. It is all rather imperfect and messy, but it is the best we have.

Narrative Voice

In the case of a novel (any novel), two questions must necessarily be asked of *any* first person narrative. First: Does the reader *trust* that the narrator gives an accurate account of what happens and a reliable and trustworthy interpretation and evaluation of its significance? Second: Is the reader convinced that the author *intends* the reader to trust the narrator? Everything is fine provided that the answers to these questions are either *both* in the affirmative or *both* in the negative because each of these alternatives implies that the text has consistency and artistic integrity. Problems occur when one of the answers is affirmative and the other negative because this implies a loss of artistic control by the author and a flawed work of art.

John is an exceptionally unreliable narrator whose credibility is always in doubt. He acknowledges it when he writes by way of preface, "Nothing in this book is true." This is why some critics have dubbed *Cat's Cradle* an 'anti-novel', for in the western literary tradition novels are associated with history. The entire book is a fabrication by Vonnegut (and, who knows, perhaps also by John) to get the reader to think about certain philosophical ideas. The story is a vehicle through which John gets the other characters to express the ideas to which Vonnegut wants the reader to give serious thought (e.g., the morality of science, the function of religion, what constitutes parenting, the nature of dictatorship, etc.).

Themes

In his book *Leviathan* (1651) the English philosopher Thomas Hobbes (1588–1679) wrote that, in the state of nature, "the life of man, solitary, poor, nasty, brutish, and short." Faced with this unattractive reality, man has contrived, in various ways, to give his existence meaning. However, if one holds that life inherently lacks meaning, this amounts to willful self-deception. The greatest such self-deception is the naïve myth of progress, the belief that society is always moving closer to perfection. In terms of the symbolism of the title, man desperately tries to see a cat and a cradle in what is simply a random and arbitrary "'tangle of string'" (12). It is man's tendency to put a filter of 'meaning' between himself and the world that Vonnegut satirizes in *Cat's Cradle*.

Technological Advancement

Writing at the time of the Cuban Missile Crisis (1962) in the context of the Cold War between USA and Russia, Vonnegut had every reason to believe that the weaponization of science would lead to the destruction of the world. Remember that the theory of the maintenance of peace in a world where the superpowers has nuclear weapons was known by the acronym M.A.D. (Mutually Assured Destruction), the idea being that neither Russia nor America would start a nuclear war in the knowledge that the other would retaliate with nuclear weapons. The Cuban Missile Crisis had come close to shattering that concept, but M.A.D. did result in the conflict between the U.S.A. and the U.S.S.R. being a Cold War rather than a shooting war. Then, an (as now), however, the greater fear was that nuclear proliferation would upset this delicate balance. This is, of course, exactly what happens with ice-nine: it falls into the hands of a petty dictator with disastrous consequences for humanity.

In Cat's Cradle, Vonnegut shows that humans are incapable of controlling the weapons of mass destruction that they have the ability to invent: the inevitability that people will misuse the power they have threatens the very survival of mankind. The scientists who invent them lack (for a variety of reasons) the moral capacity to care about the impact of their research on people. The representatives of governments are concerned only with winning the arms race. For both sets of people, ice-nine represents power, and in the novel the one thing that people want is power and they do not seem to mind what they do to get it.

The Truth of Science

Science sees itself as discovering truth and increasing human knowledge. It stands in opposition to religion which it dismisses as mere superstition and belief in magic. Vonnegut rejects the scientific idea of "pure research" producing abstract truth because in the real world the practical results of research are used to exert power over others. The scientists in the novel willfully blind themselves to this reality.

Dr. Hoenikker is responsible for two inventions which threaten the entire survival of mankind: the atom bomb and *ice-nine*, yet he treats his research as a game, blinding himself to the danger it poses to humanity.

The Lies of Religion

The military base on San Lorenzo is called "Fort Jesus." The history of the island shows that the Church has always been allied with the colonial oppressors beginning with the "butterball [i.e., well-fed] priests" who kept the people submissive under the exploitation of the Castle Sugar Company (124) and extending to the economic colonialism (capitalism) that is exemplified by the Crosbys, who want to transfer bicycle production to a country where "'they're all Christians'" and which has cheap labor and no labor laws (93).

Religion gives people elaborate lies in which to believe and in so doing, though it does not improve the material aspect of existence, it allows people to feel better about their wretched lives. In Christianity, the explanation for poverty and disease lies in Original Sin (Adam in the Garden of Eden) and hope lies in salvation (through the sacrifice of Christ on the cross). Moreover, the priests claim to know God's purpose in making things the way they are. In general, religions are as dishonest about providing truth as is science, since they present lies as truth. Bokononism is unique in that it acknowledges that everything it says is foma (e.g., The First Book of Bokonon begins, "'Don't be a fool! Close this book at once! It is nothing but foma [i.e., harmless untruths].'"

There are, however, several paradoxes in Bokononism. It is significant that the narrative includes a number of religious terms, rendered in the invented language of San Lorenzo, "all of which sound vaguely or explicitly obscene" (Morse 59). Despite its honesty about lying, it still functions as "the opium of the people" (Karl Marx) because it gives the masses a reason to continue their unhappy existence without trying to change it. Despite everything he says, the people believe Bokonon's message. As Allen points out, when ice-nine threatens to destroy the world, "The people of San Lorenzo took these events to be an act of God, rather than science, and turned to their holy figure for an explanation" (Simmons Ed. 221). They "commanded him to tell them exactly what God Almighty was up to and what they should do" (273). When he tells them another lie, they accept it as truth (an example of tragic irony) and commit suicide on mass, "even though it is clearly stated within Bokononism that any attempt to understand or to believe to understand the wishes of a higher being would be futile and foolish" (Ibid.). Thus, Bokononism is no different from any other religion since ultimately it involves the cynical manipulation of the people. The narrator explains, "These people in desperation believed that Bokonon did know the word of God, and so they followed his advice. It is not the chemical per se that caused their deaths, but their belief that the wishes of God can be known and accurately followed" (Ibid.). In allowing this to happen, Bokonon (who does not, of course kill himself) is as immoral as any scientist in the book.

[This scene reminded me of the following, "On November 18, 1978, Peoples Temple leader Jim Jones instructed all members living in the Jonestown, Guyana compound to commit an act of 'revolutionary suicide,' by drinking poisoned punch. In all, 918 people died that day, nearly a third of whom were children" (ThoughtCo. "The Jonestown Massacre").]

Religion and Science as False Panaceas

> The Apocalypse comes in *Cat's Cradle* because Science (represented by Felix Hoenikker) concentrates on progress while it ignores morality, responsibility, and Religion (represented by Bokonon) ... concentrates on happiness while it ignores the physical reality.
> (Schatt 68)

There would seem to be a dichotomy between science and religion: the former represents the triumph of reason and the latter claims to access a transcendent truth beyond human reason. For Vonnegut, however, both are equally false paths. Thomas explains that the aim of the novel is to show that, "[t]hrough Bokononism, we are admonished not to become stuck in our metaphors. But through Hoenikker, we are admonished to be wary of science without morality" (Simmons Ed. 39). The difference is epitomized by the opposite worlds of Ilium (where scientists do "pure research" to increase the fund of human knowledge) and San Lorenzo (where a cynical madman openly tells the people lies that will make them feel better about their wretched lives.) This is what Dr. Breed means when he says that science is "'the very antithesis of magic ... The exact opposite of magic" (36). Actually the difference between science and religion is more apparent than real: they each provide a façade of meaning that obscures the terrible truth that no one can make sense of life and that attempting to improve the human condition is futile.

The Futility of Art

Newt paints a cat's cradle as a symbol of the pointless of ascribing meaning to life when there is none. Julian Castle immediately sees that the painting represents "'the meaninglessness of it all,'" but by throwing Newt's painting into the waterfall, he takes it a step further: even making a commentary on the meaninglessness of life is meaningless, because the people do not learn or benefit from experience. The painting (and by extension all art and all human endeavor) is "'Garbage – like everything else'" (169).

Interpersonal Relationships

With one exception, the personal relationships described in this novel are a disaster. The three Hoenikker children suffer from their father's failure to show them any love or concern, but they go on to make their own mistakes, each one desperately trying, and failing, to find love. Abele explains, "[T]he world is destroyed not through a deliberate act of war, but through the careless handling of a military discovery, *ice-nine*. However, what has made ice-nine more dangerous than it need be is Dr. Hoenikker's failure to properly father his children" (Simmons Ed. 82). The narrator, John, is hardly more successful in his personal relationships. Twice divorced, he boasts that he has had over fifty women in his life, enjoys a one-night-stand with the prostitute Sandra, and immediately imagines himself in love with Mona, a girl he has never even met. The single exception is the Mintons, the only sympathetic and loving couple in the novel. Bokonon uses the term *duprass* to describe such a close union which seems to exempt them from the human flaws that the other characters exemplify so abundantly.

Bokonon uses the term *granfalloons* to describe the random, and therefore meaningless, groups into which people fall: John and Newt went to the same college and are in the same fraternity; Hazel Crosby feels much more comfortable among Christians, particularly if they are Hoosiers. These superficial ties are at best of no significance, but the greatest *granfalloon* is national identity because it leads to xenophobia, patriotism and ultimately war.

Free Will or Divine Control

John's narrative repeatedly questions the idea of self-determination. Writing in retrospect, he feels that he has been compelled to be in certain places, to meet certain people and to do certain things there. His experiences have led him to accept the theology of Bokononism which holds that things happen because they are *supposed* to happen, that God controls the fates of humans in ways that are ultimately unknowable. The mechanism through which God works is the *karass,* that is, the individuals that a person finds him/herself "'tangled up with ... for no very logical reason'" (2). The reason is God's will.

Since the only voice in *Cat's Cradle* is that of the narrator, it is all too easy to assume that Vonnegut also believes that humans lack the ability to determine their own destiny and therefore to avoid catastrophes such as freezing all of the water in the world and killing humanity. Is the belief that one can actually take meaningful action in the world presented as just another example of trying to see a cat and a cradle in a random pattern of string – a self-deception? John would say that it is, but then John is a (very) unreliable narrator. The whole thrust of the novel seems to assert that man *needs* to take responsibility for his actions in order to avoid global catastrophe.

18

The Will to Power

On a political and on an individual level, human life seems to be ruled by the desire for power on the assumption that power will bring happiness. Deprived of love in their childhood, Hoenikker children seek to control their lives in ways that will bring them happiness. Frank makes ants fight, seduces his friend's wife, and creates a model world that he can manipulate at will. Possession of his father's *ice-nine* allows him to bribe "Papa" Monzano so that he can use a real country for his ideas and his experiments without ever having to face the human consequences of his action. Angela, who never had a boyfriend, uses her *ice-nine* to buy a handsome husband, but finds herself locked into an unhappy marriage. Newt similarly exchanges *ice-nine* for an idyllic honeymoon on Cape Cod with a Ukrainian dancer who turns out to be a Russian spy and steals a piece of his *ice-nine*. Ultimately, *ice-nine* does not bring the Hoenikker children power, it simply makes them vulnerable to being exploited by others.

Study Guide: Notes, Questions and Commentary

This novel deserves to be read *reflectively*. The notes aim to give necessary background information. The notes explain references and allusions in the text that might not be immediately clear to a contemporary reader. The questions are *not* designed to test you but to help you to locate and to understand characters, plot, settings, issues, and themes in the text. They do not normally have simple answers, nor is there always one answer. Consider a range of possible interpretations - preferably by *discussing* the questions with others. Disagreement is to be encouraged! The commentary explores the text in depth.

Chapters 1 – 8

Notes

"Call me Jonah" (1) – The narrator's opening is a comic parody of the opening of Herman Melville's classic novel *Moby Dick* (1851), "Call me Ishmael." (Ishmael was the first, illegitimate, son of Abraham by his servant Hagar. Both he and his mother were cast out into the wilderness by Abraham.) In the Old Testament, Jonah is the prophet commanded by God, "Arise, go to Nineveh, that great city, and cry against it; for their wickedness is come up before me" (*Jonah* 1.2 KJV). Reluctant to obey, Jonah travels to other lands. In the course of his evasions he is swallowed by a large fish in whose belly he spends three days and three nights. Finally, Jonah realizes that there is no evading God's will and goes to Nineveh. By calling himself Jonah, John is making a parallel with how he came to end up in San Lorenzo.

"Hiroshima" (1) – On the morning of August 6, 1945, an American B-29 bomber (called Enola Gay) dropped the first atomic bomb (called Little Boy) on Hiroshima, a city that was a significant military and industrial part of the Japanese war effort. The explosion wiped out 90% of the city and immediately killed 70-80,000 people; tens of thousands more later died from exposure to radiation. [Three days later, another B-29 dropped a second atom bomb on Nagasaki. Estimates of those immediately killed range from 22,000 to 75,000 people.]

"Bokononist" (2) – An invented religion. (Glossaries of Bokonon terms are readily available on the Internet.)

"Republic of San Lorenzo" (2) – Do not look for it on a map: the island is an invention. It shares many social and political features with Haiti and Cuba.

"Central Park" (3) – In New York.

"Delta Upsilon" (6) – Founded in 1834, this fraternity was originally restricted to New England private universities but now has chapters throughout the U.S. and Canada. The *Delta Upsilon Quarterly*, which began publication in 1882, is the fraternity's official magazine.

"Ilium" (8) – a fictitious town in eastern New York State, used as a setting for several Kurt Vonnegut novels.

"Manhattan Project" (9) – On May 12, 1942, President F. D. Roosevelt signed an order creating a secret project to develop a nuclear weapon. It would eventually be named the Manhattan Project. Research and development was chiefly carried out in three secret scientific cities: Hanford, Washington; Oak Ridge, Tennessee; and Los Alamos, New Mexico. Probably the single most important scientist involved in the Project was nuclear physicist J. Robert Oppenheimer, the director of the Los Alamos Laboratory that designed the actual bombs.

"cat's cradle" (12) – A game that can be played by one or two people in which a long loop of string is passed around the fingers of the hands to form various cradle-like patterns or figures. Perhaps surprisingly, the game is found (under a variety of names) in cultures around the world.

"Tri-Delt" (13) – Delta Delta Delta is a prestigious international sorority for women founded in 1888 at Boston University.

"*The Saturday Evening Post*" (14) – Despite its name, this publication was founded in 1821 as a weekly magazine. In the first half of the twentieth century, it was one of the most influential magazines in the United States.

"Alamogordo" (17) – The first nuclear explosion occurred on July 16, 1945, when a plutonium implosion device was tested 210 miles south of Los Alamos at the Alamogordo Bombing Range.

"L.S.T.'s" – "Landing Ship, Tanks" (LST), or tank landing ships. We learn later that car smugglers used them to transport cars illegally to Cuba.

"Borzoi Dance Company" – A fictional company probably based on the Bolshoi Ballet (Russian for "Great Ballet") then, as now, the leading ballet company in Russia.

Questions

1. Brainstorm as many meanings as you can think of that John might have intended in the title *The Day the World Ended*. John states firmly that when he planned the book, "It was to be a Christian book. I was a Christian then" (1). Why might he be motivated as a Christian to write such a book?

2. Bokononists believe that all of humanity is organized into teams, called *karasses,* within which individuals unknowingly carry out God's will.

   - What is the point that Calypso 53 makes about the composition of *karasses*?
   - Who are the members of John's *karass* and how did he come into contact with them?

3. How can a religion based on lies be said to be "useful" (5)?

4. On the morning that the atomic bomb was dropped on Hiroshima, Dr. Hoenikker went over to his six-year-old son Newt to show him how to play cat's cradle. What had prompted Dr. Hoenikker to play the game? What about his action in relation to the game was typical and what entirely untypical of him?

5. What is the nature of the "experimenting" that Frank is doing? In what ways is Frank's action here similar to what his father does when he conducts his research?

Commentary

John sees himself (and wants the reader to see him) as Jonah because, in retrospect, he feels that a force has been guiding him, "somebody or something has compelled me to be certain places at certain times, without fail. Conveyances and motives, both conventional and bizarre, have been provided" (1). The reader does not yet know the end to which John feels himself to have been maneuvered, though he states that it all started with the idea to write a book called *The Day the World Ended*. (John tells us that the book was "never finished" [2], but, as we find out at the end of the novel, *Cat's Cradle* could equally be titled *The Day the World Ended*.) It is implied that whatever John feels that he was guided towards eventually happened on the island of San Lorenzo, and that its religion, Bokononism, allowed him to understand the whole process. Readers will find it useful to mark in their text, or to note on paper, occasions when John *appears* to be moved to be at certain places and to meet certain people by some divine force. Also, remember that John is an unreliable narrator – just because he is convinced of something does not mean that the reader has to be convinced.

Bokononism believes that all individuals are organized into "teams that do God's will" without the individuals ever understanding their part in the divine plan. Each of these teams is called a *karass*, and because God is God a *karass* can transcend "national, institutional, occupational, and class boundaries" (2-3). Bokonon explains, "'If you find your life tangled up with somebody else's life for no very logical reasons, … that person may be a member of your *karass*'" (2). No one, however, can understand God's purpose. This is the point of Bokonon's story of building the doghouse: anyone who believes that they *do* understand God (including Bokonon) is a fool – hence the title of the chapter. The "instrument" that brings a *karass* together is called the *kan-kan*. In this case, the *kan-kan* was John's idea for writing a book because this brought him into connection with the three children of Dr. Hoenikker, or as John puts it they became tangled in his *sinookas*, that is, the "tendrils of [his] life" (6). (If that sounds like a cat's cradle in which people are caught, as in a spider's web, that is probably deliberate.)

John quotes the opening sentence of *The Books of Bokonon*, "'All of the true things I am about to tell you are shameless lies'" (5). Every other religion claims to be able "to discover, to understand" God's will (4); only Bokononism openly acknowledges that this is impossible and honestly acknowledges that its main purpose is to make believers *feel* as if their lives have meaning and purpose while conventional religions dishonestly provide only the *illusion* of knowing God's meaning and purpose.

In contrast to the *karasses* into which individuals are grouped by God for some (unknowable) purpose, humans also group themselves, or allow themselves to fall into, *granfalloons* (a term that is not introduced until later in the novel). These are the superficial and random relationships that individuals form that can distract them from the real work of their *karasses*. Newt and Jonah share two *granfalloons*: they went to Cornel University and are in the same fraternity, and it is on the basis of these chance connections that John learns of Newt's existence. He refers to Newt as "*Brother*" (6), as is the custom of fellow frat members, but Newt's reply shows how insubstantial such connections are since he is being kicked out of both Cornell and his fraternity because of his poor grades.

Newt's description of Dr. Hoenikker is of a man interested only in his research, "People couldn't get at him because he just wasn't interested in people" (13-14). His father had no interest in his wife (or, after her death, in his daughter) except in so far as she looked after him. Once he even *tipped* her for breakfast, as though she were a waitress. Also, he never interacted with his children. He had no intellectual curiosity, since Newt reports that he never, "'read a novel or a short story in his whole life … didn't read his mail or magazines or newspapers'" (10). So it was natural that he never read the convict's novel titled 2000 A.D. "about how mad scientists made a terrific bomb that wiped out the whole world" (9) – which is the second book mentioned in the text that sounds very like Cat's Cradle. Instead, he played with the string in which the manuscript came bound. This provides a symbol for Dr. Hoenikker's evasion of moral responsibility for his nuclear weapons and other research. Even after the bomb had been tested and "it was a sure thing that America could wipe out a city with just one bomb," he showed no understanding of the moral implications of what he had produced. When another scientist remarked to him, "'Science has now known sin,'" he simply asked naively, "'What is sin?'" (17). After that, Dr. Hoenikker lost all interest in the bomb and moved onto other intellectual games. The indifference of scientists to the consequences of their work is one of the basic themes of the novel.

The creation of the atomic bomb dramatically increased the scale of destruction that one nation could inflict on another, but Dr. Hoenikker shows no concern for human life. This attitude seems to have been passed onto Frank who similarly shows no concern for the bugs that he pits against each other in the Mason jar. When Angela questions him, he says he is "'Experimenting,'" as tough science absolves him of responsibility. Newt joins Frank in watching the ants fight and all other thoughts, including those about his father, are overcome by his interest in the game of making them fight. When Newt writes about two girls who committed suicide by jumping into a gorge because they did not get into the sorority of their choice, he seems to have no sense of sorrow or remorse for them. He mentions it briefly and unemotionally, as a rather odd act, not as a tragic waste of life.

Angela seems to be the only member of the Hoenikker family with genuine human feelings (except perhaps her mother). After her mother's death, she looks after her father and brothers as though they are "three children" (15). She tells Newt that he has hurt his father by not being interested in the cat's cradle and slaps him for saying that he hates his father. For her pains, Frank punches her viciously in the stomach, but when she looks to her father for help all he does is stick "'his head out a window … and never even asked later what the fuss had been about'" (17). The neglect which each of the three children suffered, particularly after the death of their mother, makes them very vulnerable to being exploited by others. The story of how Newt is deceived by Zinka, who "was old enough to be Newt's mother" (20) will simply be the first example.

Chapters 9 - 23

Notes

"W. C. Fields" (25) – American comic actor (1880-1946) famous for his movie roles.

"créme de menthe" (26) – A sweet, mint-flavored alcoholic drink mainly used in cocktails.

"George Minor Moakley" (29) – A fictional character.

"Marmon" (31) – The Marmon Motor Car Company of Indianapolis, Indiana, was established in 1902 but the name disappeared in a merger in 1933. Its cars were large and luxurious.

"yellow press" (50) – The kind of newspapers that use scandalous, lurid, or sensationalized stories to attract readers (think *National Enquirer*!).

Questions

6. What is the theme of the commencement speech that Dr. Breed gives (24)? How does Breed's attitude to scientific research differ from that of Hoenikker? How does the author show that it is no more valid that Hoenikker's attitude?

7. Explain the effect achieved by having Dr. Breed tell the story of George Minor Moakley at precisely this point in the novel? Comment on the irony of Dr. Breed's attitude to George Minor Moakley.

8. Analyze the description of Dr. Breed when he tells John about the automobile accident which, ultimately, led to Emily's death. How does the reader know that he really did love her (though not whether that love was returned)?

9. Why does John comment at the end of Chapter 18, "Had I been a Bokononist then, that statement would have made me howl"? Howl with laughter or with anger? What fault would a Bokononist find with Dr. Breed's statement about "'truth'" (41)?

Commentary

John writes that, one year later, "another story [we never discover what it was] carried me through Ilium" (20). This is another indication of a force compelling him "to be certain places at certain times" (1), as is the fact that Sandra and the bartender had gone to school with Franklin. Like his father, brother and sister, Frank seems to have been a social isolate. Sandra reports, "'He never got on any committee, never played any game, never took any girl out'" (21). His sole interest seems to have been model-making – an impression that later turns out to be erroneous.

The main themes of this section are the dangers of scientific research and the complete disconnect between scientists and ordinary people. The representatives of science are the self-involved Dr. Hoenikker, the defensive

Dr. Breed, and the incomprehensible Dr. Horvath; the representatives of the ordinary people are the prostitute Sandra, the two barmen, the Girl Pool, and Miss Pefko. Despite Dr. Breed's claims to the contrary, neither Hoenikker nor Horvath make any effort to communicate their ideas and Miss Pefko appears to lack the intelligence and the motivation even to try to understand.

When he gave the commencement speech for Dr. Hoenikker (who failed to appear), Dr. Breed showed a naïve faith in science. Sandra reports that he said, "'The trouble with the world was … that people were still superstitious instead of scientific. He said if everybody would study science more, there wouldn't be all the trouble there was.'" Vonnegut mocks the claim of science to (as Breed claimed), "'discover the basic secret of life someday'" (24). Sandra "dutifully" tries to remember Breed's point, and the bartender not only remembers it but recalls that he recently read that scientists had actually found the secret of life. The joke is that all the bartender and Sandra know is that it is, "'something about protein'" (25). They have no idea *what* about protein and there is no indication that this discovery will improve their lives in any way. Ironically, their deep faith in, even reverence for, something that they do not understand means that for people like them science *is* a form of religion, a superstitious belief in magic.

This theme is also exemplified in Francine Pefko, a secretary at the Research Laboratory, who is of the opinion that scientists think too much. She has no understanding of the ideas that she types out, and says of her boss Dr. Horvath, "'here he's maybe talking about something that's going to turn everything upside-down and inside-out like the atom bomb'" (34). Dr. Breed's confidence that Dr. Horvath is very good at explaining and that Dr. Hoenikker said that "'any scientist who couldn't explain to an eight-year-old what he was doing was a charlatan'" rings hollow because there is no evidence that either man ever even tried to explain (34). The fact that Dr. Breed is out of touch with real people is confirmed when he admits to his secretary, Miss Foust, that buying chocolate for the girls in the Girl Pool "'slipped [his] mind.'" He simply does not regard the girls as people, telling John that they "'belong to anybody with access to a dictaphone'" (38). The girls are like nuns; they only leave their cloister at Christmas to sing carols and get their gift of chocolate.

Science for Dr. Breed is the hope of the world, the triumph of rationalism and the antithesis of religion, superstition and magic. His advocacy for "pure research" involves an oxymoron: like Dr. Hoenikker, he does not even consider that scientists must carry moral responsibility for the outcomes of their research. The kind of abstract knowledge which he says is the goal of science is a myth. John admits that "Every question I asked [Dr. Breed] implied that the creators of the atom bomb had been criminal accessories to murder most foul." Sensing John's hostility, Dr. Breed accuses him of believing that "'scientists are heartless, conscienceless, narrow boobies, indifferent to the fate of the rest of the human race..."' (39). However, Dr. Breed's defense of "pure research" rather proves John's point since it is not intended for any practical purpose that will improve human life but simply to create, "'New knowledge'" which Dr. Breed calls, "'the most valuable commodity on earth. The more truth we have to work with, the richer we become'" (41). His attitude is contrasted with that of his son who quit his job at the Research Lab on the day the bomb was dropped telling the barman, "'anything a scientist worked on was sure to wind up as a weapon ... Said he didn't want to help politicians with their fugging wars anymore'" (26). Dr. Breed is appalled by the fact that George Minor Moakley literally sang on the scaffold that "'He wasn't sorry about anything.'" Breed exclaims. "'Think of it! ... Twenty-six people he had on his conscience!'" (29). Of course, the atom bomb killed tens of thousands, but neither Hoenikker nor Breed (who was, at least technically, his supervisor) feel any conscience about that. Dr. Breed is, however, obviously very moved when he tells John about the accident which, ultimately, led to Emily's death. It seems that he can respond emotionally to an individual he cares about, but not the mass of humanity.

The origin of ice-nine is described. A Marine general came to Dr. Hoenikker with the problem of mud and the Doctor did what he always did. Dr. Breed tells John that Dr. Hoenikker approached the problem, "'in his playful way'" and that he "'always approached old puzzles as though they were brand new'" (43). Breed's description of the concept of ice-nine is interrupted by the beautiful carol singing of the Girl Pool. John comments:

> I am not likely to forget very soon their
> interpretation of the line:
> "The hopes and fears of all the years are here
> with us tonight." (47)

Readers are expected to notice that the Girl Pool gets the line wrong. It should be, "The hopes and fears of all the years are met in thee [i.e., Christ] tonight." This slip of the tongue implies that scientists have become God since they hold the fate of the world in their hands. It also foreshadows that *ice-nine* will have graver consequences for mankind that neither Dr. Breed nor John could at that time imagine. John, however, does grasp that if the *ice-nine* seed were ever used there would be no stopping the freezing process. He gets an exasperated Dr. Breed to admit that using *ice-nine* just once "'would be the end of the world!'" (50). Fortunately, Breed assures John that *ice-nine* "'does not exist'" (49).

When it comes to science, the Hoenikker children have no more understanding than the average person. Unlike the average person, their deprived upbringing has left them desperately longing for both love and power since as children they were unloved and powerless. Their inheritance of the only sample of *ice-nine* is dangerous because they have no real understanding of both how it works and what consequences it might have for the population of the world.

Chapters 24 – 34

Notes
"M.I.T." (66) – The Massachusetts Institute of Technology.
"Duco Cement" (70) – A multi-purpose household glue that is still available.

Questions
10. If ice-nine is the "waxing" (*wampeter*) of the *karass* in which John now understands himself to be, what is the "waning" *wampeter* (52)?

11. When his taxi driver asks to take a "brief detour" to the monument salesroom, John says he "agreed with some peevishness" but that had he then been a Bokononist he "would have agreed gaily to go anywhere anyone suggested" (63). Explain the difference between the two mindsets.

12. What is the effect on John of finding his own name on the pedestal of the angel in the monument store (73)? Connect your explanation to the Bokononist concept of *vin-dit*.

Commentary
Dr. Breed's argument that pure research is about finding new knowledge and truth (41) is undercut by Miss Faust's memory of Dr. Hoenikker once betting her that she "'couldn't tell him anything that was absolutely true.'" She replied, "'God is love,'" offering a religious conception of truth [Bokononism, of course, denies the validity of religious truth], but Hoenikker rejected her 'truth' as irrational and unscientific. He asked, "'What is God? What is love?'" (55). These are, of course, very different questions. The first is theological and valid given that men have answered it in many different ways. The second, however, is about a basic human feeling that he appears never to have experienced. Lacking an emotional tie to other humans, he is unwilling and unable to consider the moral implications of his work, that is, the ways in which his research will impact the lives of actual people. Breed's position is further undermined by the plaque on the wall outside Dr. Hoenikker's laboratory which states:

THE IMPORTANCE OF THIS ONE MAN IN THE
HISTORY OF MANKIND IS INCALCULABLE.

This statement is not intended to be ironic, but it is, for the atomic bomb killed tens of thousands of people – it is literally not possible to calculate the number accurately. The plaque also makes explicit the link between pure research and real-world consequences that Dr. Breed has consistently sought to deny. By creating ice-nine, of course, Dr. Hoenikker virtually put an end to human history, so that the conclusion of the novel makes the statement on the plaque a massive understatement!]

John's dominant impressions of Dr. Hoenikker's laboratory are that "The old man had left the laboratory in a mess" and that there is a "quantity of cheap toys lying around" so that even "the pieces of conventional laboratory equipment ... seemed drab accessories to the cheap, gay toys" (56). Once again Hoenikker's childish irresponsibility is stressed. On his desk is a photograph of a war memorial with "the names of villagers who had died in various wars." For a moment, John thinks that this must be the reason for the photograph being on Hoenikker's desk (i.e., that at some level Hoenikker actually *did* understand the human implications of weapons research), but Miss Faust tells him that Hoenikker was interested in "'how [the] cannonballs are stacked on different courthouse lawns,'" adding, "'Apparently how they have got them stacked in that picture is very unusual'" (57). Obviously, this is related to Dr. Breed's earlier explanation of how water freezes. In both cases, it is evident that there is no such thing as pure scientific research in pursuit of abstract truth. The photograph juxtaposes technological advancement (the cannon balls) with its real-world consequences (the names of the dead) – a link that Dr. Hoenikker never made.

Ironically, the Hoenikker children used their father's Nobel Peace Prize money to buy an impressive tombstone for their mother on which they wrote poems expressive of their love for her. Marvin comments that they visited the monument often and that "'those kids got more consolation out of that than anything else money could have bought'" (65). Dr. Hoenikker may have had a huge (though not a positive) impact on mankind, but the two monuments show the relative importance of mother and father in the lives of their children. Because Marvin, unlike the research scientists, has come into contact with death and with grieving people, he is one of the few characters who recognizes the unhappiness of the Hoenikker children.

In conversation with Marvin Breed, John calls Nobel Prize money "'Dynamite money'" and explains that Alfred Nobel made his fortune from the invention of dynamite. Nobel thus stands as one man who *did* see the connection between scientific discovery and human suffering – albeit too late. Marvin Breed articulates for the first time the contradiction between the supposed innocence of Dr. Hoenikker ("'harmless and gentle and dreamy ... so innocent he was practically a Jesus – except for the Son of God part...'" [67]) and the man who "'couldn't even be bothered to do anything when ... his own wife, was dying for lack of love and understanding.'" He asks rhetorically the same question John's narrative has been posing, "'[H]ow the hell innocent is a man that helps make a thing like the atomic bomb?'" (68). [A rhetorical question is a statement in the form of a question. The question requires no answer because the answer is implied.

Chapters 35 – 43

Notes

"American Flyer" (76) – a brand of model railroad manufactured by the A. C. Gilbert Company, 1938–1966.

"Madonna" (80) – the Virgin Mary.

"barracuda" (81) – a large ferocious fish found in tropical and subtropical oceans.

"Chris-Craft" (82) – a privately owned, Florida-based manufacturer of recreational powerboats.

"Fata Morgana" (83) – a mirage seen just above the horizon of the ocean.

"Dr. Albert Schweitzer" (84) – The French-German theologian, organist, philosopher, and physician (1875 – 1965) opened a hospital at Lambarene in the jungle of Equatorial Africa 1913. He won the 1952 Nobel Prize for Peace.

"Tommy Manville" (84) – a Manhattan socialite and millionaire (1894-1967) who had 13 marriages to 11 women and was a celebrity because of the extravagance of his lifestyle.

"Barbara Hutton" (84) – an American socialite, heiress and philanthropist (1912-1979) who was also noted for her extravagant lifestyle.

"pissant" (89) – an insulting term for a person who is insignificant and/or contemptible – a peasant.

"Daughters of the American Revolution" (92) – to become a member, you must have an ancestor who helped contribute to securing the independence of the United States of America.

"International Order of Odd Fellows" (92) – an international benevolent fraternity begun in London in 1730 and in the U.S.A. in 1819.

"Harry Truman" (94) – Truman (1884-1972) became President of the U.S.A. on the death of F. D. Roosevelt and served as the 33rd President of the United States from 1945 to 1953.

Questions

13. Jack tells John that his wife just left him and that he is, "'still trying to put the strings of [his] life back together'" (74). This is a bit of a cliché. Can you relate it to the title of the novel? [It might help to consider John's description of Frank's model, "And everywhere ran a spaghetti pattern of railroad tracks" (75).]

14. What similarities are there between Frank's work on his model of a country and his father's work in the field of science? What significant differences are there?

Commentary

The impressive model of a "fantastic little country" (74) that Frank made in the basement of Frank's Hobby Shop shows his obsessive desire to have something over which he could have complete control. Frank seems to have devoted his life to his model to the exclusion of personal relationships – much like his father. Its existence foreshadows the attraction which San Lorenzo has for him since there he is in charge of the San Lorenzo Master Plan for "new roads, rural electrification, sewage-disposal plants, hospitals, clinics, railroads – the works" (81). What is missing from his job description is, of course, people whom he never meets. In San Lorenzo, Frank is modeling on a grand scale. He is, indeed, as "Papa" Monzano calls him, "'the blood son of Dr. Felix Hoenikker'" (82).

Jack seems genuinely to have liked Frank and admired his astonishing creativity for building models. He regrets not having been able to finance his education and particularly laments his supposed death telling John, "'I wonder if those dirty sons of bitches ... have any idea what it was they killed!'" (77). This eulogy (which in many ways recalls the tributes to Dr. Hoenikker, for example on his plaque) is ironic on a number of levels. The reader later discovers both that Frank spent so much time at the Hobby Shop because he was having sex with Jack's wife (presumably the same one who has just left Jack) and that he himself gave his portion of *ice-nine* to the dictator of San Lorenzo in return for power and privilege. The boy who made insects fight in a bottle is the same teen who created a perfect model world while betraying Jack, and the same young man who tries to do to the real world what he did with his model of it. He is as vain, self-centered, and careless of the impact of his actions on others, as was his father.

The incident in which his apartment is "wrecked by a nihilistic debouch" in the form of Sherman Krebbs is taken by John to be another example of divine control of his destiny. Krebbs is a *wrang-wrang*, that is "a person who steers people away from a line of speculation by reducing that line ... to an absurdity" (78). In this case, Krebbs effectively ends any temptation John might be feeling to regard life as meaningless. (Nihilism means the rejection of all religious and moral principles in the belief that life is meaningless; truth does not exist and everything is arbitrary.)

That John is sent to San Lorenzo to interview Julian Castle is another example of something happening, as Bokonon would say, "'As it was *supposed* to happen'" (84), though John did not realize it at the time. Julian Castle, an American sugar millionaire, is used by Vonnegut to parody accepted ideas about what constitutes moral conduct. Opening a charity hospital gains him international acclaim and accolades for his philanthropy, but his wealth was based on exploitation of the native people by the Castle Sugar Corporation. For most of his adult life he was noted for his "lechery, alcoholism, reckless driving, and draft evasion." John adds damningly, "He had a dazzling talent for spending millions without increasing mankind's stores of anything but chagrin [irritation, resentment, anger]" (84).

On the 'plane to San Lorenzo, John meets a politician (Minton, the newly-appointed ambassador) and a capitalist (Crosby, the bicycle-manufacturer). Neither of them is attractively presented. The former seems cynical and will not "bubble about anything" (87); the latter is "of the opinion that dictatorships were often very good things" and feels that people were put on earth "to build bicycles for him" (92). Lowe wants to move his business to San Lorenzo because there are no laws that ensure that employers pay their workers a living wage and provide decent and safe working conditions. H. Lowe and Hazel Crosby represent the ignorance and greed of American capitalists who wish to impose their own values, religion and culture on others with no respect for cultural diversity. Hazel is only comfortable with people who are exactly like herself, which essentially means Christian Hoosiers! She has no comprehension that other cultures might have other beliefs and values which they hold as firmly as she does her own. She represents American xenophobia at its worst. H. Lowe favors dictatorships because they offer stability for American firms wishing to relocate production to places with low-wage economies. His defense of the use of the hook to eliminate crime, and his support for capital punishment at home, suggests his brutal indifference to poverty. He represents American nationalism at its worst.

Chapters 44 - 55

Notes

"Senator McCarthy" (98) – Joseph Raymond (Joe) McCarthy (1908-1957) was a Senator for Wisconsin for the last ten years of his life. He led a campaign against what he saw as Communist infiltration in the highest levels of American society. He remains a controversial figure. Vonnegut would agree with Mr. Welch who famously said, on June 9, 1954, during the Army-McCarthy Hearings: "You've done enough. Have you no sense of decency, sir, at long last? Have you left no sense of decency?"

"Charles Atlas" (102) – born Angelo Siciliano (1892-1972), he was a bodybuilder who marketed his 'Dynamic Tension' program by mail order – the concept was that a person could build muscle by opposing one muscle against another and so did not need gym equipment.

"Saint Augustine" (103) – Aurelius Augustinus (354-430) was a theologian whose writings had a tremendous influence on the development of the medieval Church.

"Blackbeard ... Edward Teach" (103) – pirate captain (c. 1680-1718) who operated in the Caribbean and along the East Coast of America and is supposed to have buried his treasure on an island off the coast of Georgia – it has never been found.

"the second Battle of Ypres" (105) – battle in World War I fought from April 22 – May 25, 1915, for control of the town of Ypres in western Belgium that saw the first mass use by Germany of poison gas on the Western Front – Allied casualties were almost 90,000 killed, wounded or missing.

"Rumfoord Estate" (106) – fictional estate that occurs again in Vonnegut's novel *The Sirens of Titan*.

"Mohandas K. Ghandi" (106) – a prominent leader of India's independence movement in the 1930s and 1940s, employing non-violent civil disobedience to oppose British rule.

"Basque" (108) – language spoken by natives of the Basque Country, a region around the western end of the Pyrenees on the coast of the Bay of Biscay partly in France and partly in Spain – its people have long struggled for independence from both of these countries.

"Hyannis" (114) – largest of the seven villages in the town of Barnstable, Massachusetts.

"Fabri-Tek" (116) – there is a Fabritek Company in Winchester, Virginia – the company in the novel seems to be a front for weapons manufacture.

"a *Wehrmacht* engineer" (118) – a member of the Nazi armed forces in World War II.

Questions

15. In his account of Claire Minton's letter and the trouble that it caused her husband, what is Vonnegut saying about the mistake that Americans make in their foreign policy? Another way of asking the same question is: What criticism is Vonnegut making of the concept of 'American exceptionalism'? (You may remember, or may have read, that after the terrorist attacks of 9/11, or indeed after just about any terrorist attack against Americans, people asked, 'Why do they hate us?)

16. Explain how the concept of 'Dynamic Tension' has been embodied in the political and social structure of San Lorenzo.

17. Explain why, in Chapter 51, John refers to Newt as, "The little son of a bitch" (111).

Commentary

The reader learns that Minton was once suspected of having Communist sympathies. Claire Minton says that she was to blame because in a letter to *The New York Times* she wrote that "'Americans can't imagine what it is like to be something else, to be something else and proud of it'" (97). In writing that, Mrs. Minton was questioning the prevailing political dogmatism. In the wake of World War II, America saw itself as having saved the world for democracy, and, believing that its own values were superior to all others, Americans would not tolerate opposition either in other countries or at home. Those who questioned American exceptionalism were most often labeled 'communists': there were assassinations of foreign leaders (e.g., the Iranian Prime Minister Mohammad Mossadegh in 1953 and Patrice Lumumba, the first legally elected prime minister of the Democratic Republic of the Congo in 1961) and persecution of 'communists' and 'fellow travelers' at home. The key point is that failure to empathize with others pretty much summarizes what is wrong with most of the characters in the novel. (This analysis is obviously controversial, though the facts stated *are* facts. Vonnegut interpreted events from a left-wing perspective. Political conservatives would take a very different view of the same events. Research the history and come to your own conclusions.)

The earlier impression that Angela, alone among the Hoenikker children, is capable of empathy turns out to be false. When he meets her on the flight to San Lorenzo, John comments that she "persisted in treating Newt like an infant … Angela was a God-awfully insensitive woman, with no feeling for what smallness meant to Newt" (111-112). She seems to love her father, for example, by protecting his reputation. She tells John that in his book he "'better make Father a saint, because that's what he was'" (112). It is interesting that she uses religious language to describe her father and her own feelings about him: she is like a Christian revering a saint. Science is, at least for her, the new religion. Her irrational faith in her father ignores all of the evidence in the novel that he was completely egocentric, incapable of empathizing with others, and without a moral conscience. Angela does not love her father but the false image of her father that she has created to cope with his emotional coldness to, and exploitation of, her (i.e., she is in denial). She herself remains indifferent to the consequences of her father's research insisting that, "'Actually, the day [the bomb was dropped on Hiroshima] was just like a regular day'" (112). It is as though she has completely blanked out the death and destruction caused by the bomb.

Ironically, the Hoenikker children are just as selfish as their father. Having been starved of love and happiness as children, they have each traded *ice-nine* to buy both and in doing so they have placed all life on earth at great risk. Like Dr. Hoenikker, they give no thought to the awful implications their actions hold for mankind. John draws attention to the irresponsibility of Newt and Angela when he points out that (though he did not know it at that time) each is carrying *ice-nine* on the plane, just as Frank took *ice-nine* on the boat to San Lorenzo, "The little son of a bitch had a crystal of ice-nine in a thermos bottle in his luggage, and so did his miserable sister, while under us was God's own amount of water, the Caribbean Sea" (111). The anger and bitterness of John's language in this quotation is evident. (I am reminded of Nick Carraway's verdict on Tom and Daisy, "I couldn't forgive him [Tom] or like him, but I saw that what he had done was, to him, entirely justified. It was all very careless and confused. They were careless people, Tom and Daisy – they smashed up things and creatures and then retreated back into their money or their vast carelessness, or whatever it was that kept them together, and let other people clean up the mess they had made" [*The Great Gatsby* by F. Scott Fitzgerald].)

Chapters 56 – 66

Notes

"Hernando Cortez" (125) – Spanish conquistador (1485-1547) who brought down the Aztec empire.

"Tum-bumwa" (126) – a fictional dictator.

"Simón Bolívar" (133) – the Venezuelan military leader (1783-1830) who was instrumental in the revolutions against the Spanish Empire that established independence in several South American countries.

"major domo" (141) – the person who manages things for the person who is in charge.

Questions

18. Examine the idea that San Lorenzo is a symbol for life anywhere on earth. What does Vonnegut appear to be saying about the nature of human activity?

19. John is head over heels in "love" with Mona. That makes him a very unreliable narrator wherever he is writing about her. What negative aspects of her character, persona and situation does he appear not to see?

Commentary

The story of San Lorenzo's past is the history of human futility. It has been colonized by a number of European countries, but everyone who has ever occupied it has found it impossible to generate any profit from the barren soil creating a vicious circle in which the only people who suffer are the native inhabitants who have been exploited by a succession of rulers. John comments, with more than a touch of Bokononist philosophy, "God, in His Infinite Wisdom, had made the island worthless" (125). For this reason, no one has ever wanted to defend San Lorenzo.

The description of the economic exploitation of San Lorenzo by Castle Sugar is a comic version of colonial exploitation as it occurred throughout the undeveloped world. The dark comedy lies in the fact that Castle Sugar never turned a profit but "by paying laborers nothing … managed to break even year after year, making just enough to pay the salaries of the workers' tormentors" (124). John is describing a meaningless, vicious circle which ignores the impact of its activity on those it exploits. It is implied that the rich Catholic Church was complicit in all of this. When the idealists McCabe and Johnson (Bokonon) decided to divide the country's income equally between all adults, Philip Castle's book reports, "'each share came to between six and seven dollars'" (147). They did not try that again!

Speaking of being abandoned by Zinka, Newt says, "'She broke my heart. I didn't like that much. But that was the price. In this world, you get what you pay for'" (128). Zinka's "price" for appearing to love Frank was Newt's portion of *ice-nine*, but he shows neither regret nor remorse for the danger to which he has exposed the world in allowing *ice-nine* fall into Russian hands. Like his siblings, he has used the bargaining power of *ice-nine* to gain purely selfish ends (related to his deprived childhood) with no concern for the consequences. The first sight of San Lorenzo reveals it to be "an amazingly regular rectangle" (132) which recalls the description of Frank's model in Jack's shop as "a fantastic little country built on plywood, an island as perfectly round as a township in Kansas" (74). The parallel makes it clear that Frank, who once exerted his need for control over insects and inanimate objects, is now playing the same 'game' with the lives of real people.

The way in which the dictator "Papa" Monzano exploits the supposed enemy Bokonon is similar to the way in which the Party exploits the image of Goldstein in George Orwell's novel *Nineteen Eighty-Four*. The welcoming ceremony is as orchestrated as anything in Orwell's novel: the people are completely cowed and lifeless. They expect nothing from these visitors – nothing that will improve the wretched condition of their lives. Like many of the 'Third World' dictatorships that replaced European colonialism, the dictator of San Lorenzo lives in luxury and ensures that comfortable, modern conveniences are provided for foreign visitors, yet nothing is done to improve the conditions of the people.

While Bokonon has been established as the public enemy, the image of Mona has been manipulated to be the erotic-innocent symbol of the Republic. It is hard to judge Mona since we see her only through the eyes of John who is immediately infatuated with her. However, she seems to be a rather compliant tool of the island's ruler. When "Papa" collapses at the reception ceremony, John notes that Mona, "was still serene and had withdrawn to the rail of the reviewing stand. Death, if there was going to be death, did not alarm her" (145).

"Papa" nominates Frank as his successor because, as he says publically, "'Science – you have science. Science is the strongest thing there is'" (146). This appears to be strange at first because Frank never was a scientist. What the reader does not yet know is that "Papa" is speaking of Frank having brought *ice-nine* (which is weaponized science) to the island.

Chapters 67 – 73

Notes

"bubonic plague" (160) – the same disease we call The Black Death that decimated the population of Medieval Europe in the fourteenth century.

Questions

20. Make a list of the examples of human failure in this section.

Commentary

Speaking of the wreck of the Greek ship whose mutinous crew "'didn't know how to run her and smashed her on the rocks'" (a fitting symbol for the futility of human effort in this world) Philip Castle comments, "'some people got free furniture, and some people got bubonic plague'" (a fitting symbol for the arbitrary nature of happiness and suffering in this world). In his jungle hospital, Julian Castle worked tirelessly to help the sick, but was so helpless to do so that once the bulldozer got stuck in the corpses. Finally, struck by the ludicrousness of his position as a doctor quite unable to help his patients, Philip reports that his father "'started giggling'" and could not stop (162). Then he said to Philip, ""'Son ... someday this will all be yours'"" (162). This cynical, even nihilistic, act of benediction expresses the sense of futility that future generations will inevitably suffer in their attempts to improve the lot of mankind. Each generation leaves only a mess of failure behind: progress is a myth. Philip Castle's empty hotel seems to be yet another symbol of that failure, since it has only ever had three guests and two of them he has insulted. The mosaic of Mona is another fruitless exercise since she is unattainable, either because Philip is, as Claire Minton believes, homosexual (122), or because she is just about to be engaged to Frank.

Chapters 74 – 81

Notes
"impasto" (164) – a painting technique: paint is applied very thickly so that the brush or painting-knife strokes are visible.
"Meade Lux Lewis" (180) – Anderson Meade Lewis (1905-1964) was an American musician in the boogie-woogie style.

Questions
21. What went wrong with the plan of McCade and Bokonon to rule San Lorenzo using the principal of 'Dynamic Tension'?

22. What does Newt mean by his repeated rhetorical questions, "'See the cat? See the cradle?'"

23. What similarities do you find between Newt's painting and Angela's playing of the clarinet?

Commentary
On his taxi ride to Frank's house, John comments on the "scenes of hideous want" through which he is driven (163). In contrast, the house itself (which recalls the architecture of Frank Lloyd Wright) is opulent. The servant, Stanley, is "the first plump San Lorenzan" John has seen (164). This graphically illustrates the economic divide between the rulers and the ruled.

John describes Newt's painting as "scratches [that] formed a sort of spider's web … the sticky nets of humanity hung up on a moonless night to dry" (164). He identifies it as the spider web in which mankind inevitably becomes entangled. Newt identifies his painting as a cat's cradle – the game that his father played as the atomic bomb was dropped. The game is a perfect symbol of the meaninglessness of all human pursuits because there is no cat and there is no cradle in the abstract arrangement of strings. Nevertheless, as Newt says, "'For maybe a hundred thousand years or more, grownups have been waving tangles of string in their children's faces,'" just as his own father did (165). Children have thus been presented with a lie about the nature of human life, the lie being that it *is* possible to perceive order in what is actually chaos. Julian Castle agrees with Newt about the pointlessness of life. He says, "'Man is vile, and man makes nothing worth making, knows nothing worth knowing'" (169). To illustrate his point he tosses Newt's painting into the waterfall. So much for art!

Julian tells John that Bokonon "'cynically and playfully, invented a new religion'" (172). The reader recalls that playfulness was a feature of Dr. Hoenikker's approach to scientific theories. The only difference is that Bokonon actually did want to make the people happier, and since he could not achieve that end in material terms he did it by psychological manipulation, "Truth was the enemy of the people, because the truth was so terrible, so

Bokonon made it his business to provide the people with better and better lies" (172). Life became what John calls "'a work of art'" (175) which worked well enough in raising the happiness of the people until first McCabe and then "Papa" Monzano took the whole charade seriously and then, as Julian says, "'people really did start dying on the *hy-u-o-ook-kuh*'" (175).

Angela's sense of grievance resurfaces. She complains about her father's meager salary (which came to the not inconsiderable sum of $28,000 a year – a lot of money in those days), which is pretty insensitive given that she is surrounded by the poverty of San Lorenzo. Vonnegut juxtaposes her complaints about the injustice of her father's salary with Julian's description of the nets in which poor people downstream of Frank's house catch his scraps. It is Newt who fills John in on the real cause of Angela's unhappiness: her handsome husband, the one she 'bought' with *ice-nine*, is chronically unfaithful to her. She has made no better deal with her *ice-nine* than did Newt himself. As he tells John, "'See the cat? See the cradle?'" (179), by which he means that human happiness (whether that of his siblings or the people of San Lorenzo) is a lie that people tell themselves.

Angela's playing explores the same hell as Newt's painting. John, who is impressed, comments, "Such music from such a woman could only be a case of schizophrenia or demonic possession" (182). Both Newt and Angela make art out of their despair at the meaninglessness of life. In contrast, Julian Castle appears to believe in the worthiness (or at least the utility) of Bokononism, since he admits to finding the practice of *boko-marum* indispensible in running his hospital and is always quoting from The *Books of Bokonon*. Perhaps in revenge for Julian's destruction of his painting, Newt repeats, "'See the cat? … See the cradle?'" (183) by which he means that all religion is a meaningless lie – even a religion that admits that it is a meaningless lie, because that admission is simply a cynical ploy.

Chapters 82 – 99

Notes
"Auschwitz" (186) – Nazi Germany's largest camp (actually a complex of camps) located in southern Poland – over one million people were exterminated there.

"Chicago stockyards" (189) – for over a century from 1865, Chicago was the largest meat processing area in the world – American poet Carl Sandburg called Chicago, "hog butcher for the world."

"oubliette" (214) – a secret room (often a cell or dungeon) accessed through a trapdoor.

"Western Hemisphere University of the Bible of Little Rock" (215) – no such institution exists but private universities offering degrees by correspondence (these days on-line) do exist – many such 'universities' were simply bogus at the time this novel was written.

"*Popular Mechanics*" (215) – a magazine that has been published continuously since the first edition January 11, 1902 – it deals with science and technology in ways non-specialists can understand.

Question
25. When Frank tries to persuade John to take the position of President he talks in clichés (overused, worn out expressions). Make a list of the ones he uses. Now explain *why* he uses so many.

Commentary
Dr. Koenigswald, like Julian Castle, is working at the jungle hospital in order to make some sort of restitution for the sins of his earlier life. In this case, he was a physician at Auschwitz concentration camp where he was responsible for the deaths of tens of thousands of innocent people, mainly Jews. Julian himself points to the futility of Koenigswald's effort to wipe out the sins of his past (and therefore of his own efforts) when he comments that, though Koenigswald is "'saving lives left and right,'" it will take him until 3010 to save as many people as he allowed to be killed.

When the soldiers come to Frank's house with orders to protect the next President, John tells them, "'He isn't here now'" (188). This is an example of dramatic irony, for most readers will have worked out that Frank intends John to be the next President of San Lorenzo. Another example of dramatic irony comes when, following the restoration of electrical power, John "hilariously" asks Angela and Newt why they have rushed from their rooms each carrying "little Thermos jugs, identical red-and-gray jugs capable of holding about three cups of coffee" (192). To John, their action is inexplicably absurd, but then (unlike the reader) he does not know that Newt and Angela are carrying their *ice-nine*. (Unless I have misunderstood, there is a plot problem here because I was under the impression that Zinka stole Newt's *ice-nine* and took it back to Russia with her.)

Frank has used his *ice-nine* to get himself a position of affluence and power in which he does not have to take any human responsibility for his actions. His safety is, of course, endangered by "Papa's" illness and by the dictator's choice of Frank to succeed him. Therefore, he is desperate to pass the position of president to anyone else who will take it. Talking to John, Frank comes close to honesty when he says, "'I know my limitations ... They're the same limitations my father had ... I've got a lot of very good ideas, just the way my father did ... but he was no good facing people, and neither am I'" (198). This is true as far as it goes, but it equates moral indifference with shyness and in doing so glosses over the psychological defect he shares with the rest of his family. It is a mute point how good either Dr. Hoenikker's or Newt's ideas actually are: they seem to have added to the sum of human misery rather than reducing it. Even now, Frank is guilty of placing "the destiny of thousands upon thousands of persons" in the hands of "a fogbound child [John]" (199) simply for his own convenience.

Frank has lived his life in bitterness against his father and his peers who taunted him with the name "Secret Agent X-9." He had no conscience about cheating on Jack (who, we remember, liked and helped him), just as he has no conscience about the way he has exploited the people of San Lorenzo. Notice that he tells John, "'I was screwing Jack's wife every day'" (201). The language is brutal: this is not a confession; it is a boast. At this point, however, John seems to be just as bad. He accepts the presidency partly because he feels he does not have the free will to refuse it and partly out of sexual desire for Mona whom he hardly knows. John's decision is no more morally defensible than the decisions made by anyone else in the novel, including Mona who appears to be entirely passive and without any critical faculties at all. Her credo is, "'It is not possible to make a mistake'" which may be good Bokononism but is a very irresponsible way to live (203).

John seeks to impose on Mona a monogamy that he himself has certainly not followed. He calls himself "a man of the world, having had, by a reckoning I once made, more than fifty-three women" (204), yet he seeks to have all of her love for himself. In imposing his male values on Mona, he is showing that he does not understand or respect either her or her beliefs. He finally accepts her love of others, and her right to perform *boko-maru* with whomever she wants only because she says she will not marry him. He is motivated by lust not love.

John has the same illusions about the Presidency as McCade and Bokonon had when they first came to San Lorenzo. They were convinced that they could turn the island into a Utopia (127) and he is convinced that he will "chop down the hook" and "be a firm, just, and kindly ruler, and that my people would prosper." Looking back he realizes that such dreams were 'Fata Morgana. Mirage!' (213). On his deathbed, "Papa" will say that it, "'Doesn't matter … who is President …'" (217), presumably because whoever is in power will not change anything for the better because that is simply not possible.

The account of the Last Rites of Bokononism includes that religion's creation myth. In some ways, it is the same as the creation myth in *Genesis*, but there is no Fall of Man. Life is an honor and everything God created is interesting. Life, in this myth, is a positive experience and death, the natural end to life, is nothing to be feared. If this is all lies (as Bokonon admits that it is) then it is lying with the intention of making people feel better about their lives. That is the very opposite of what science seems to do as Dr. Koenigswald says when he tells John, "'I am a very bad scientist. I will do anything to make a human being feel better, even if it is unscientific. No scientist worthy of the name could say such a thing'" (219).

"Papa" officially puts his faith in John and Frank to teach his people science because "'Science is magic that *works*'" (218). The novel shows the reverse. That is why, at the end of his life, "Papa" declares himself "'a member of the Bokononist faith'" (218). Neither science nor religion do any practical good for mankind, but science does make things worse and religion does make people feel irrationally better about their lives. Ironically, Dr. Hoenikker created *ice-nine* as a solution to the problem of mud. In the light of the Bokonon creation myth, the solution was to kill all life.

Chapters 100 – 109

Note

"andiron" (236) – one of a pair of metal supports used to hold wood burning in a fireplace.

Questions

26. Of the three Hoenikker children, Frank is the most like his father. How is this shown in these chapters?

27. What is wrong with Mona?

28. Compare and contrast the ways in which the three Hoenikker children react to John's accusation that they are responsible for the end of the world.

Commentary

As soon as John is effectively (though not officially) President, Frank makes an "abrupt abdication … from all human affairs" (223). John realizes that by accepting the Presidency he has "freed Frank to do what he wanted to do more than anything else, to do what his father had done: to receive honors and creature comforts while escaping human responsibilities" (224-225). In turn, John realizes that, since he has no power to actually make the lives of the people better, he has to maintain the charade of "good in the jungle, and evil in the palace" (226).

John has an idealistic view of his profession, writing. He tells Philip Castle, a fellow writer, "'When a man becomes a writer, I think he takes on a sacred obligation to produce beauty and enlightenment and comfort at top speed'" (231). This sounds like the same idealistic nonsense that Dr. Breed spouts about science; it sounds like religious devotion. The reader recalls that, during the course of the narrative, John has written absolutely nothing; he is no better than the scientists whom he has criticized. See the cat? See the cradle?

At the reception in the castle, John sees Mona objectively for the first time. Noting her passive indifference, he asks himself whether it represents "the highest form of female spirituality" or is a sign that she is "anesthetized, frigid – a cold fish, in fact, a dazed addict of the xylophone, the cult of beauty, and *boko-maru*." He decides to follow the teaching of Bokonon it is better to lie to himself about Mona and consider her "sublime" (233).

The effigies floating in the harbor represent the evil rulers of the world, each responsible for the deaths of millions of people: the leaders of Communism and Fascism and the German Kaiser who began World War I. The symbolic destruction of these caricatures of evil, the central event of the Hundred Martyr festival, is an assertion that man has the ability to learn from history and to rule more humanely in the interests of the people. Ironically, of course, San Lorenzo is itself ruled by a dictator whether that person's name is

McCabe or "Papa". It is the ultimate irony that one of the planes meant to destroy these caricatures of evil will set off the accident that leads to worldwide catastrophe.

Following the discovery of "Papa's" suicide, and the subsequent death of Dr. Koenigwald, John confronts the three Hoenikker children with the reckless selfishness of what they have done. Newt's reaction is to throw up; Angela's reaction is to blame Frank; and Frank's reaction is to "'clean up this mess'" (241). Frank, however, is the only one to acknowledge some degree of responsibility, though what he says sounds more like self-justification. He tells Angela, "'I bought myself a job, just the way you bought yourself a tomcat husband, just the way Newt bought himself a week on Cape Cod with a Russian midget!'" (243)

Chapters 110 – 114

Note
"reticule" (249) – a woman's small handbag, originally netted with a drawstring and decorated with embroidery or beading. (The similarity to a cat's cradle is deliberate.)

Questions
29. Is the reader supposed to take Ambassador Minton's speech seriously? How do you know?

30. Comment on the ironic contrast between the intention of the air display and what it actually does.

Commentary
John asks, "'What hope can there be for mankind … when there are such men as Felix Hoenikker to give such playthings as *ice-nine* to such short-sighted children as almost all men and women are?'" (245). Dr. Hoenikker had been playing "puddy games in the kitchen with water and pots and pans and *ice-nine*" and then he dies leaving the *ice-nine* for his children to find (247). When it came to appropriating the *ice-nine*, the Hoenikker children did not say "anything to justify their taking *ice-nine* as their personal property … there was no talk of morals" (251). Their actions exemplify the complete disconnect between science and moral thinking that has been a major theme of the novel.

Ambassador Minton's speech is a protest against war and against the patriotic celebration of the sacrifice that men make in war. It is by a long way the most humane, positive and hopeful statement of values in the novel. Patriotism groups people into *granfalloons,* to defend which they are willing to die, and ceremonies such as the present one represent a denial of the irrational senselessness of war. Wars, he says, represent "'the stupidity and viciousness of all mankind'" because they represent the lowest form of animal greed in man (254). It is, John notes, "a strikingly Bokononist speech" (253), but this is only partly true, for Minton still has faith that man can learn from the past and do better by "'working consciously and tirelessly to reduce the stupidity and viciousness of ourselves and of all mankind'" (255). However, such idealism has been consistently shown to be empty rhetoric by the event of the novel and even as he concludes his speech, the six planes of the San Lorenzan Air Force, whose aim is to "shoot the effigies of … 'practically every enemy that freedom ever had'" come into view (256). As Morse concludes:

> The picture of the Mintons themselves disappearing into Ice-9 bears out Vonnegut's notion that although Ice-9 was nonsense, it did enjoy "a certain moral validity" … The good, loving Mintons – who see themselves as an

integral part of the human community – perish because of the greed, stupidity, and isolation of Hoenikker and his children that unleashed Ice-9 upon an unsuspecting world. (38)

Chapters 115 – 127

Notes

"peristalsis" (261) – the involuntary constriction and relaxation of a muscle.

"Sterno stove" (263) – a form of camping stove.

"the rack and the peddiwinkus and the iron maiden" (264) – three instruments of torture – the rack is a machine that pulls a body apart; the peddiwinkus involves being hung from the ceiling by the wrists with a heavy iron ball tied to each foot; and the iron maiden encloses a body inside an iron cabinet with a hinged front and spike-covered interior.

"*The Book of Knowledge*" (270) – perhaps refers to *Cassell's Book of Knowledge* an eight-volume encyclopedia which was first published in 1922.

"corona" (271) – a circle of light.

Questions

32. Lots of people commit suicide in this section. Explain their motivation. Explain why Bokonon doesn't commit suicide.

Commentary

All of the characters in the novel are what E. M. Forster termed 'flat characters':

> Flat characters ... in their purest form ... are constructed round a single idea or quality; when there is more than one factor to them, we get the beginning of the curve toward the round. The really flat character can be expressed in one sentence such as, "I will never desert Mr Micawber." There is Mrs Micawber - she says she won't desert Mr Micawber; she doesn't, and there she is.
> (*Aspects of the Novel* [1927])

None of the characters, including the narrator, change at all following the catastrophe: Frank Hoenikker is interested in how ants survived *ice-nine* while ignoring entirely his role in freezing the entire world, and Hazel's desire to create an American flag shows her continuing allegiance to nationhood, patriotism, and neo-colonization. Morse concludes, "there appears no new beginning for humans but only for a handful of ants" (37).

Paradoxically, Bokononism offers the only meaningful way of understanding life, but Bokonon himself gives in to the will of the people and becomes a mass murderer. Bokononism is absolutely right in criticizing man's need to be given a reason for life, an explanation of existence. In its myth of creation, God bluntly tells man that He will not provide an answer; man must create a reason for life. Earlier, John had the following conversation with Frank:

"What is sacred to Bokononists?" I asked after
a while.
"Not even God, as near as I can tell."
"Nothing?"
"Just one thing."
I made some guesses. "The ocean? The sun?"
"Man," said Frank. "That's all. Just man."
(211)

Fairly self-evidently, Frank does not live by this belief any more than did his
father. However, the final irony is that Bokonon does not live by it either. He
still believes in the existence of a God, but nevertheless finds no deep meaning
behind the destruction of the Earth. He regards it as the culmination of "a
history of human stupidity" (287), so he has no faith in man either. That is why,
when the people of San Lorenzo capture him, desperate to be told "exactly what
God was up to and what they should do," he cynically tells them that God
wants them "to have the good manners to die" (273). That is, he lies to them,
knowing that he lies to them, and they gullibly accept what he says as divine
and commit mass suicide.

The SparkNotes Editors take a much more positive view of Bokononism:

> Bokonon, despite his skepticism, did not
> exhibit the careless, indifferent nihilism of
> Julian Castle. Neither did he exhibit the vain,
> irresponsible, greedy, self-deluded ignorance
> of the Hoenikker children and John. Bokonon
> as a character is very much like Vonnegut. In
> the face of the never-ending problem of human
> indifference, stupidity, pride, and ignorance, he
> could do nothing but laugh, just as Vonnegut
> uses his humor to encourage his readers to
> laugh even as they read about humanity's
> unflattering characteristics.

This interpretation need to be carefully considered, particularly since it is
supported by so perceptive a commentator as Morse who writes:

> The invented *Books of Bokonon* form a moral
> core for the novel that Vonnegut uses to
> comment on and/or to provide counterpoint to
> the action. In an otherwise mad whirling
> world, Bokonon – along with John the naïve
> narrator – helps establish a positive set of
> values so necessary for the success of this
> apocalyptic satire. These positive values
> include a belief in the sanctity of human

beings, the necessity of human love, the
primacy of human community, and a vision of
a world larger than a single person, family or
country. (63)

I do find those values in the novel, but I cannot equate them with either the narrator John or with a man who says that his final verdict on existence would, if he were younger, be to swallow ice-nine and "make a statue of myself, lying on my back, grinning horribly, and thumbing my nose at You Know Who" (287). There *are* many aspects of Bokonon's criticism of the way humanity seeks for meaning that are spot on, but the theology of Bokononism is faulty because it still *is* a theology: it does not deny that God is in control, merely that God's will is knowable to man. The search for transcendent meaning whether through belief in a deity or belief in a scientist (or a political system, or an economic system, or an ideology, etc.) is an illusion, but that is not the same thing as saying that life is necessarily meaningless. The truth is that each of us is able to create meaning by the way that we live.

Annotated Works Cited

Vonnegut, Kurt. *Cat's Cradle*. 1963. New York City: Dial Press, 2010. Print.

Morse, Donald. *The Novels of Kurt Vonnegut: Imagining Being an American*. Westport: Praeger, 2003. Print.
   (An excellent survey of Vonnegut's longer fiction that does not separate the novels into distinct chapters. Therefore, I would recommend reading the whole book.)

"The Nobel Prize in Chemistry 1932". *Nobelprize.org*. Nobel Media AB 2014. Web. 6 May 2017.

Patterson, Kellee. Kissel, Adam ed. "*Cat's Cradle* Study Guide". *GradeSaver*. 14 April 2006. Web. 4 May 2017.
   (A valuable site from which I learned a lot.)

Schatt, Stanley. *Kurt Vonnegut, Jr*. Boston: Twayne Publishers, 1976. Print.
   (Contains a helpful section on the novel.)

Simmons, David. Ed., *American Literature Readings in the 21st Century: New Critical Essays on Kurt Vonnegut*. New York: Palgrave Macmillan, 2009. Print.
   (Several essays touch on Cat's Cradle. The final essay, by Claire Allen, is most helpful.)

SparkNotes Editors. "SparkNote on *Cat's Cradle*". *SparkNotes.com*. SparkNotes LLC. n.d.. Web. 28 Apr. 2017.
   (A valuable site from which I learned a lot.)

Summary Notes

The following notes draw together different themes in the novel.

The Myth of Progress

Cat's Cradle is a satire (i.e., it uses of humor to expose and criticize people's stupidities). From *The Fourteenth Book of Bokonon*, "'What Can a Thoughtful Man Hope for Mankind on Earth, Given the Experience of the Past Million Years?' ... 'Nothing'" (245). "'History!' writes Bokonon. 'Read it and weep!'" (252)

SCIENCE:

Science elevates rationalism over everything else. The target of the novel is the arrogance of scientists: they are cut off from society; they fail to improve human life; and they lack a moral conscience over consequences for mankind of their discoveries.

Dr. Hoenikker – a child, playing, ego-centric – entirely incapable of empathy or love – blind to morality – "'Science has known sin.' And do you know what Father said? He said, 'What is sin?'" (17).

Dr. Breed – the idealist who believes that there is such a thing as pure research which adds to humanity's store of truth and knowledge – for him science is "the very antithesis of magic ... The exact opposite of magic" (36).

Dr. Horvath – the man who makes no effort to explain – Miss Pefko says, "'it's just like a foreign language ... he's maybe talking about something that's going to turn everything upside down'" (34).

RELIGION:

Religion elevates the truth of faith over everything else. The target of the novel is the arrogance of those who believe that they can see and understand God's plan: they fail to materially improve the lives of people and claim to find meaning in the world's suffering.

The "butterball" (i.e., well fed) priests of San Lorenzo – lived much better lives than the miserable people to whose spiritual needs they were supposed to minister – "The San Lorenzo Cathedral, dynamited in 1923, was generally regarded as one of the man-made wonders of the New World" (124) – McCabe and Johnson threw the priests out.

The Episcopalian lady in Newport – "claimed to understand God and His ways perfectly" (4), but could not understand the blueprint for a doghouse.

Bokononism – "Truth was the enemy of the people, because truth was so terrible, so Bokonon made it his business to provide the people with better and better lies" (172) – Bokononism works in the same way that all religions work except that it makes no secret of its being built on lies – nevertheless, the people believe it – their belief leads to mass suicide, "The mountebank told them that God was surely trying to kill them, possibly because he was through with them, and that they should have the good manners to die" (273).

GOVERNMENT

Government elevates the state or a political philosophy above everything else. The target of the novel is the arrogance and selfish self-aggrandizement of those who exploit the people for their own ends and fail to materially improve the lives of people.

Colonialism – San Lorenzo is ruled by a succession of European nations: France, Denmark, Holland, England, and Spain – "The people of San Lorenzo had nothing but diseases, which they were at a loss to treat or even name" (123).

Economic colonialism – Castle Sugar (1916-1922) establishes plantation feudalism, "'by paying laborers nothing for their labor, the company managed to break even year after year, making just enough money to pay the salaries of the workers' tormenters" (124).

Dictatorship – Emperor Tum-bumwa, a "'maniac'" who 'killed' 1,400 people building pointless defenses – McCabe and Johnson (1922) who set out to make "San Lorenzo a Utopia" (127), but "failed to raise the people from misery and muck" (133), and both went insane.

Nationalism/Patriotism – Kaiser Bill and the First World War

Fascism/Communism – Hitler, Mussolini, Karl Marx, Stalin (the Second World War), Mao, Castro (Dictatorship) – "'practically every enemy that freedom ever had'" (230).

The Cold War/Arms Race – The invention of the atom bomb triggers an arms race between USA and Russia – both get their hands on *ice-nine*.

American exceptionalism – Claire Minton, "'Americans couldn't imagine what it was like to be something else, to be something else and proud of it … Americans … are forever searching for love in forms it never takes, in places it can never be'" (97) – for this the Minton's were accused of being Communists.

War – Many characters in the novel have direct experience of war – Ambassador Minton says of the Hundred Martyrs, "'what killed them … [was] the stupidity and viciousness of all mankind … when we remember wars, we should take off our clothes and paint ourselves blue and … grunt like pigs'" (254). He's right.

ART

Elevates the truth of art above everything else – The target of the novel is the arrogance of the artist who seeks to find meaning and value in existence – Julian Castle, "'Man is vile and man makes nothing worth making, knows nothing worth knowing'" (169).

John is a writer – idealistic, "When a man becomes a writer, I think he takes on a sacred obligation to produce beauty and enlightenment and comfort at top speed'" (231) – but he has written nothing – the reality of the world is incompatible with artistic idealism.

Newt is a painter – Julian Castle, "'So this is a picture of the meaninglessness of it all! I couldn't agree more'" and then he throws it into the waterfall saying, "'Garbage – like everything else'" (169).

Angela is a clarinetist – "She improvised ... went from liquid lyricism to rasping lechery to the shrill skittishness of a frightened child, to a heroin nightmare. Her glissandi spome of heaven and hell and all that lay in between" (181-182).

The Hoenikkers: A Psychologically Damaged Family

What each of these characters has in common is the failure to acknowledge and confront reality.

Felix Hoenikker

- – incapable of empathy/love
- – immature and childish
- – totally egocentric
- – morally unaware

Emily Hoenikker

- – self-sacrificing
- – may have been unfaithful (?)

Angela Hoenikker

- – physically unattractive
- – starved of love and attention
- – compensates by idealizing her father – "'He's one of the greatest men who ever lived'" (16) – "'He just wasn't very demonstrative'" (115) – "'the book … better make Father a saint because that's what he was'" (112)
- – self-sacrificing (leaves high school to look after three 'children')
- – expresses her misery by playing the clarinet –
- – attempts to use *ice-nine* to buy love (a handsome, but unfaithful, husband)

Franklin Hoenikker

- – starved of love and attention
- – compensates by: making ants fight just to observe the results; sleeping with Jack's wife; building a model world that he can control; and running away as soon as his father dies
- – attempts to use *ice-nine* to buy power without personal or moral responsibility
- – separates ideas from their consequences – morally unaware

56

Newt Hoenikker

– physically deformed – four-foot midget

– starved of love and attention

– traumatized by the incident of the cat's cradle on the day the world ended

– attempts to use *ice-nine* to buy love (Zinka the midget dancer who turns out to be a thief and a Russian agent)

– expresses his misery by painting

The Central Symbol of the Novel

"'He tried to play with me … he went down on his knees … he waved that tangle of string in my face. 'See? See? See?' he asked. See the cat's cradle? See where the nice pussycat sleeps? Meow. Meow' … I burst into tears. I jumped up and I ran out of the house …" (12)

"Newt's [painting … consisted of scratches … [that] formed a sort of spider's web … I did not wake the midget who had made this dreadful thing … 'It's a cat's cradle … One of the oldest games there is …'" (164-165)

"'From the way she talked,' I said, 'I thought it was a very happy marriage' "Little Newt held his hands six inches apart and he spread his fingers. 'See the cat? See the cradle?'" (179)

"Little Newt snorted. 'Religion! … See the cat?' asked Newt. 'See the cradle?'" (183).

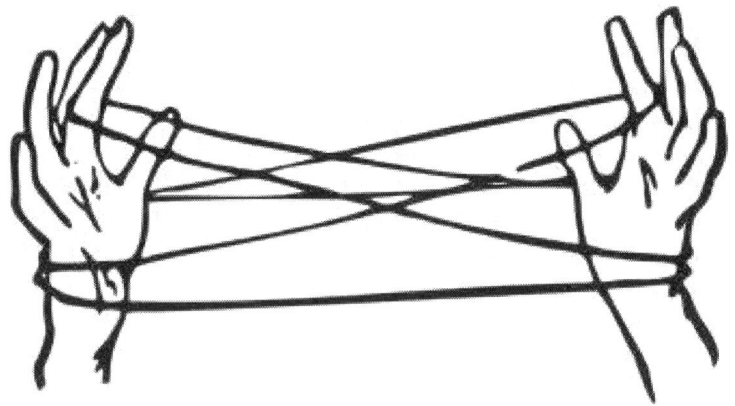

Man tries to impose meaning on what is inherently meaningless:

"Newt held out his painty hands as though a cat's cradle were strung between them. 'No wonder kids grow up crazy. A cat's cradle is nothing but a bunch of X's between someone's hands, and the little kids look and look and look at all those X's … *'No damn cat, no damn cradle.'*" (165-166)

Literary terms

Allegorical: a story in which the characters, their actions and the settings represent abstract ideas (often moral ideas) or historical/political events.

Ambiguous, ambiguity: when a statement is unclear in meaning – ambiguity may be deliberate or accidental.

Analogy: a comparison which treats two things as identical in one or more specified ways.

Antagonist: a character or force opposing the protagonist.

Antithesis: the complete opposite of something.

Authorial comment: when the writer addresses the reader directly (not to be confused with the narrator doing so).

Climax: the conflict to which the action has been building since the start of the play or story.

Colloquialism: the casual, informal mainly spoken language of ordinary people – often called "slang."

Comic hyperbole: deliberately inflated, extravagant language used for comic effect.

Comic Inversion: reversing the normally accepted order of things for comic effect.

Connotation: the ideas, feelings and associations generated by a word or phrase.

Dark comedy: comedy which has a serious implication – comedy that deals with subjects not usually treated humorously (e.g., death).

Dialogue: a conversation between two or more people in direct speech.

Diction: the writer's choice of words in order to create a particular effect.

Equivocation: saying something which is capable of two interpretations with the intention of misrepresenting the truth.

Euphemism: a polite word for an ugly truth – for example, a person is said to be sleeping when they are actually dead.

Fallacy: a misconception resulting from incorrect reasoning.

First person: first person singular is "I" and plural is "we".

Foreshadow: a statement or action which gives the reader a hint of what is likely to happen later in the narrative.

Form of speech: the register in which speech is written – the diction reflects the character.

Frame narrative: a story within which the main narrative is placed.

Genre: the type of literature into which a particular text falls (e.g. drama, poetry, novel).

Hubris: pride – in Greek tragedy it is the hero's belief that he can challenge the will of the gods.

Hyperbole: exaggeration designed to create a particular effect.

Image, imagery: figurative language such as simile, metaphor, personification etc., or a description which conjures up a particularly vivid picture.

Imply, implication: when the text suggests to the reader a meaning which it does not actually state.

Infer, inference: the reader's act of going beyond what is stated in the text to draw conclusions.

Irony, ironic: a form of humor which undercuts the apparent meaning of a statement:

   Conscious irony: irony used deliberately by a writer or character;
   Unconscious irony: a statement or action which has significance for the reader of which the character is unaware;
   Dramatic irony: when an action has an important significance that is obvious to the reader but not to one or more of the characters;
   Tragic irony: when a character says (or does) something which will have a serious, even fatal, consequence for him/ her. The audience is aware of the error, but the character is not;
   Verbal irony: the conscious use of particular words which are appropriate to what is being said.

Juxtaposition: literally putting two things side by side for purposes of comparison and/ or contrast.

Literal: the surface level of meaning that a statement has.

Melodramatic: action and/or dialogue that is inflated or extravagant – frequently used for comic effect.

Metaphor, metaphorical: the description of one thing by direct comparison with another (e.g. the coal-black night).

   Extended metaphor: a comparison which is developed at length.

Microcosm: literally 'the world is little' – a situation which reflects truths about the world in general.

Mood: the feelings and emotions contained in and/ or produced by a work of art (text, painting, music, etc.).

Motif: a frequently repeated idea, image or situation in a text.

Motivation: why a character acts as he/she does – in modern literature motivation is seen as psychological.

Narrator: the voice that the reader hears in the text – not to be confused with the author.

Frame narrative /story: a story within which the main story is told (e.g. *Heart of Darkness* by Conrad begins with five men on a boat in the Thames and then one of them tells the story of his experiences on the river Congo).

Oxymoron: the juxtaposition of two terms normally thought of as opposite (e.g. the silent scream).

Parable: a story with a moral lesson (e.g. the Good Samaritan).

Paradox, paradoxical: a statement or situation which appears self-contradictory and therefore absurd.

Pathos: is pity, or rather the ability of a text to make the audience or reader feel pity.

Perspective: point of view from which a story, or an incident within a story, is told.

Personified, personification: a simile or metaphor in which an inanimate object or abstract idea is described by comparison with a human.

Plot: a chain of events linked by cause and effect.

Prologue: an introduction which gives a lead-in to the main story.

Protagonist: the character who initiates the action and is most likely to have the sympathy of the audience.

Pun: a deliberate play on words where a particular word has two or more meanings both appropriate in some way to what is being said.

Realism: a text that describes the action in a way that appears to reflect life.

Rhetoric: any use of language designed to make the expression of ideas more effective (e.g. repetition, imagery, alliteration, etc.).

Role: A character's function in the narrative.

Sarcasm: stronger than irony – it involves a deliberate attack on a person or idea with the intention of mocking.

Satire, Satiric: the use of comedy to criticize attack, belittle, or humiliate – more extreme than irony.

Setting: the environment in which the narrative (or part of the narrative) takes place.

Simile: a description of one thing by explicit comparison with another (e.g. my love is like a red, red rose).

   Extended simile: a comparison which is developed at length.

Style: the way in which a writer chooses to express him/ herself. Style is a vital aspect of meaning since how something is expressed can crucially affect what is being written or spoken.

Suspense: the building of tension in the reader.

Symbol, symbolic, symbolism, symbolize: a physical object which comes to represent an abstract idea (e.g. the sun may symbolize life).

Themes: important concepts, beliefs and ideas explored and presented in a text.

Third person: third person singular is "he/ she/ it" and plural is "they" – authors often write novels in the third person.

Tone: literally the sound of a text – How words sound (either in the mouth of an actor or the head of a reader) can crucially affect meaning/

Tragic: King Richard III and Macbeth are both murderous tyrants, yet only Macbeth is a *tragic* figure. Why? Because Macbeth has the potential to be great, recognizes the error he has made and all that he has lost in making it, and dies bravely in a way that seems to accept the justice of the punishment.

Literary Terms Activity

As you use each term in the study guide, fill in the definition of the term and include an example from the text to show how it is used. The first definition is supplied. Find an example in the text to complete it.

Term	Definition Example
antithesis	*the complete opposite of something.*
dialogue	
foreshadow	
image, imagery	
imply, implication	

Term	Definition
	Example
irony, ironic	
dramatic irony	
tragic irony	
literal	
metaphor, metaphorical	
motivation	

Term	Definition
	Example
narrates, narrator	
narrative	
oxymoron	
paradox, paradoxical	
perspective	
plot	

Term	Definition
	Example
protagonist	
rhetoric	
role	
symbol, symbolic, symbolism, symbolize	
themes	

Appendix 1: How I Used the Study Guide Questions

Although there are both closed and open questions in the Study Guide, very few of them have simple, right or wrong answers. They are designed to encourage in-depth discussion, disagreement, and (eventually) consensus. Above all, they aim to encourage students to go to the text to support their conclusions and interpretations.

I am not so arrogant as to presume to tell teachers how they should use this resource. I used it in the following ways, each of which ensured that students were well prepared for class discussion and presentations.

1. Set a reading assignment for the class and tell everyone to be aware that the questions will be the focus of whole class discussion the next class.

2. Set a reading assignment for the class and allocate particular questions to sections of the class (e.g. if there are four questions, divide the class into four sections, etc.).
In class, form discussion groups containing one person who has prepared each question and allow time for feedback within the groups.
Have feedback to the whole class on each question by picking a group at random to present their answers and to follow up with class discussion.

3. Set a reading assignment for the class, but do not allocate questions.
In class, divide students into groups and allocate to each group one of the questions related to the reading assignment the answer to which they will have to present formally to the class.
Allow time for discussion and preparation.

4. Set a reading assignment for the class, but do not allocate questions.
In class, divide students into groups and allocate to each group one of the questions related to the reading assignment. Allow time for discussion and preparation.
Now reconfigure the groups so that each group contains at least one person who has prepared each question and allow time for feedback within the groups.

5. Before starting to read the text, allocate specific questions to individuals or pairs. (It is best not to allocate all questions to allow for other approaches and variety. One in three questions or one in four seems about right.) Tell students that they will be leading the class discussion on their question. They will need to start with a brief presentation of the issues and then conduct a question and answer session. After this, they will be expected to present a brief review of the discussion.

6. Having finished the text, arrange the class into groups of 3, 4 or 5. Tell each group to select as many questions from the Study Guide as there are members of the group.

Each individual is responsible for drafting out a written answer to one question, and each answer should be a substantial paragraph.

Each group as a whole is then responsible for discussing, editing and suggesting improvements to each answer, which is revised by the original writer and brought back to the group for a final proof reading followed by revision.

This seems to work best when the group knows that at least some of the points for the activity will be based on the quality of all of the answers.

Graphic Organizer

Plot graph

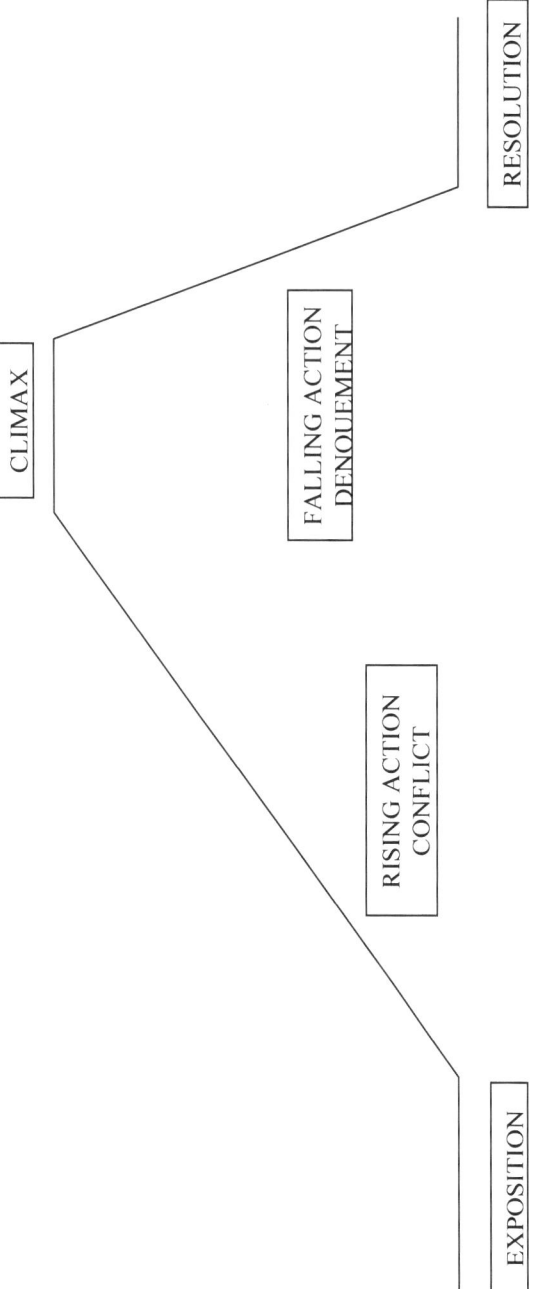

RESOLUTION

CLIMAX

FALLING ACTION
DENOUEMENT

RISING ACTION
CONFLICT

EXPOSITION

To the Reader

Ray strives to make his texts the best that they can be. If you have any comments or question about this book *please* contact the author through his email: **moore.ray1@yahoo.com**

Visit his website http://www.raymooreauthor.com

Also by Ray Moore:

Books are available from amazon.com and from barnesandnoble.com as paperbacks and some from online eBook retailers.

Fiction:

The Lyle Thorne Mysteries

Each book features five mysteries from the Golden Age of Detection:

> *Investigations of The Reverend Lyle Thorne*
> *Further Investigations of The Reverend Lyle Thorne*
> *Early Investigations of Lyle Thorne*
> *Sanditon Investigations of The Reverend Lyle Thorne*
> *Final Investigations of The Reverend Lyle Thorne*
> *Lost Investigations of The Reverend Lyle Thorne*

Non-fiction:

The *Critical Introduction series*

This is written for high school teachers and students and for college undergraduates. Each volume gives an in-depth analysis of a key text:

> *"The Stranger" by Albert Camus: A Critical Introduction* (Revised Second Edition)
> *"The General Prologue" by Geoffrey Chaucer: A Critical Introduction*
> *"Pride and Prejudice" by Jane Austen: A Critical Introduction*
> *"The Great Gatsby" by F. Scott Fitzgerald: A Critical Introduction*

The Text and Critical Introduction series

This differs from the Critical introduction series as these books contain the original text and in the case of the medieval texts an interlinear translation to aid the understanding of the text. The commentary allows the reader to develop a deeper understanding of the text and themes within the text.

> *"Sir Gawain and the Green Knight": Text and Critical Introduction*
> *"The General Prologue" by Geoffrey Chaucer: Text and Critical Introduction*
> *"The Wife of Bath's Prologue and Tale" by Geoffrey Chaucer: Text and Critical Introduction*
> *"Heart of Darkness" by Joseph Conrad: Text and Critical Introduction*
> *"The Sign of Four" by Sir Arthur Conan Doyle Text and Critical Introduction*
> *"A Room with a View" By E.M. Forster: Text and Critical Introduction*
> *"Oedipus Rex" by Sophocles: Text and Critical Introduction*
> *"Henry V" by William Shakespeare: Text and Critical Introduction*

A Study Guide

Study guides - listed alphabetically by author
* denotes also available as an eBook
NOTE Amazon has recently required Study Guides to reflect the nature of the book so eBooks are titled "Study Guide on …."

"ME and EARL and the Dying GIRL" by Jesse Andrews: A Study Guide
"Pride and Prejudice" by Jane Austen: A Study Guide
"Moloka'i" by Alan Brennert: A Study Guide
"Wuthering Heights" by Emily Brontë: A Study Guide*
"Jane Eyre" by Charlotte Brontë: A Study Guide *
"The Myth of Sisyphus" by Albert Camus: A Study Guide
"The Stranger" by Albert Camus: A Study Guides
"The Myth of Sisyphus" and "The Stranger" by Albert Camus: Two Study Guides *
Study Guide to "Death Comes to the Archbishop" by Willa Cather
"The Awakening" by Kate Chopin: A Study Guide
"The Meursault Investigation" by Kamel Daoud: A Study Guide
"Great Expectations" by Charles Dickens: A Study Guide *
"The Sign of Four" by Sir Arthur Conan Doyle: A Study Guide *
"The Wasteland, Prufrock and Poems" by T.S. Eliot: A Study Guide
"The Great Gatsby" by F Scott Fitzgerald: A Study Guide
"A Room with a View" by E. M. Forster: A Study Guide
"Looking for Alaska" by John Green: A Study Guide
"Paper Towns" by John Green: A Study Guide
"Catch-22" by Joseph Heller: A Study Guide *
"Unbroken" by Laura Hillenbrand: A Study Guide
"The Kite Runner" by Khaled Hosseini: A Study Guide
"A Thousand Splendid Suns" by Khaled Hosseini: A Study Guide
"Go Set a Watchman" by Harper Lee: A Study Guide
"On the Road" by Jack Keruoac: A Study Guide
"Life of Pi" by Yann Martel: A Study Guide *
Study Guide on "The Invention of Wings" by Sue Monk Kidd
"The Secret Life of Bees" by Sue Monk Kidd: A Study Guide
"Esperanza Rising" by Pam Munoz Ryan: A Study Guide
"Animal Farm" by George Orwell: A Study Guide
Study Guide on "Nineteen Eight-Four" by George Orwell
"Selected Poems" by Sylvia Plath: A Study Guide *
"An Inspector Calls" by J.B. Priestley: A Study Guide
"The Catcher in the Rye" by J.D. Salinger: A Study Guide
"Where'd You Go, Bernadette" by Maria Semple: A Study Guide
"Henry V" by William Shakespeare: A Study Guide
Study Guide on "Macbeth" by William Shakespeare
"Othello" by William Shakespeare: A Study Guide *

Cat's Cradle by Kurt Vonnegut

"Antigone" by Sophocles: A Study Guide *
"Oedipus Rex" by Sophocles: A Study Guide
"Cannery Row" by John Steinbeck: A Study Guide
"East of Eden" by John Steinbeck: A Study Guide
"Of Mice and Men" by John Steinbeck: A Study Guide *
"The Grapes of Wrath" by John Steinbeck: A Study Guide
"The Goldfinch" by Donna Tartt: A Study Guide
"Walden; or, Life in the Woods" by Henry David Thoreau: A Study Guide
"The Bridge of San Luis Rey" by Thornton Wilder: A Study Guide *
A Study Guide on "The Book Thief" by Markus Zusak

Study Guides available as e-books:
A Study Guide on "Heart of Darkness" by Joseph Conrad:
A Study Guide on "The Mill on the Floss" by George Eliot
A Study Guide on "Lord of the Flies" by William Golding
A Study Guide on "Nineteen Eighty-Four" by George Orwell
A Study Guide on "Henry IV Part 2" by William Shakespeare
A Study Guide on "Julius Caesar" by William Shakespeare
A Study Guide on "The Pearl" by John Steinbeck
A Study Guide on "Slaughterhouse-Five" by Kurt Vonnegut

New titles are added regularly.

Teacher resources:

Ray also publishes many more study guides and other resources for classroom use on the 'Teachers Pay Teachers' website:

http://www.teacherspayteachers.com/Store/Raymond-Moore

42588614R00044